tasks for teacher education

a reflective approach

coursebook

rosie tanner and catherine green

To Mari & Hugo and Jaś & Steve with love

Acknowledgments

Thanks to all the trainees and teachers, known and anonymous, who experienced many of these tasks in Brazil, Chile, Colombia, the Czech Republic, France, the Netherlands, Poland, the UK and the US.

In the Netherlands, thanks to trainees from the Hogeschool Windesheim for experiencing many tasks in the pilot stage, giving Rosie feedback on them and learning from them. Thanks in particular to trainee piloters Henri Hendricks, Killy van der Kolk, Monique de Jong, Stéfanie Leunissen, Harm Kramer, Rob Kroon, Remon Pauwels, and Bettina Witteveen. Special thanks to Marjolein Gritter, who gave us precise feedback from a trainee's point-of-view. Thanks to colleagues Jan Mulder, Jos Reinders, Gert Stegeman and Wim Stegenga for reading draft units and for their patience.

In the US, special thanks to Carol Breeding for trying out our tasks and motivating us to keep on right to the end, to Karen Carlisi, Jon Felperin, and Kitty Purgason for their lasting interest in the project, and to Bonnie Tangalos for her inspiring feedback. To teacher trainees in the University of California at Berkeley (UCB) Extension program, many thanks for welcoming new and different material. To colleagues at UCB Extension English Language Program in San Francisco and at LinguaTec, in Sunnyvale, thanks for generously giving Catherine valuable input and feedback.

In Bogota, Colombia, special thanks goes to Tina Castillo for her unbridled enthusiasm about our process and product. In the Czech Republic, thanks to Phil Brabbs and in Recife, Brazil, thank you to the DOTE trainees who questioned some tasks and to their trainers Eddie Edmundson, Steve Fitzpatrick and Sidney Pratt, who were supportive of our ideas.

At Longman, thanks especially to Maria Stebbings, who supported us with enthusiasm and belief in our project through three births – our book and our sons – almost without flinching. Thanks to Maria and to Sally McGugan for their helpful and continuing feedback during the time leading up to publication. Finally, many thanks to Judith Greet for helping us to complete the project.

Pearson Education Limited
Edinburgh Gate, Harlow
Essex CM20 2JE, England
and Associated Companies throughout the world.

www.longman.com

© Addison Wesley Longman Limited 1998

The rights of Catherine Green and Rosie Tanner to be identified as authors of this Work have been asserted by them in accordance with the Copyright, Designs and Patents Act 1988

First published by Addison Wesley Longman Limited 1998
Fourteenth impression 2011
Sei in ITC Stone Serif 10/13pt and Frutiger Light 10/12pt
Printed in Malaysia, PJB
Designed by Neil Adams
Illustrations by Chris Pavely

ISBN 978-0-582-31663-8

Acknowledgements
We are grateful to the following for permission to reproduce copyright material:

Addison Wesley Longman Ltd for 'error' definition from Longman Dictionary of Applied Linguistics, Longman 1995; EMI Songs Ltd, London WC2H 0EA for the lyrics to the song 'Why?', words and music by Tracy Chapman. © 1988, EMI April Music Inc/Purple Rabbit Music, USA; Mary Glasgow Magazines for an extract from the article 'Reading tasks with magazines' by Clare Lavery from Practical English Language Teaching, Vol 12, no 2, December 1991; Teachers of English to Speakers of Other Languages (TESOL) and the authors for an extract from p67 in Dialogue Journal Writing with Non-native Speakers, by Joy Kreeft Peyton and Leslee Reed, 1990 Alexandria, VA: TESOL. Copyright 1990 by TESOL.

Photo Acknowledgements
We are grateful to the following for permission to use copyright photographs:

Ace Photo Agency/Benelux Press for page 103 bottom right, /Anthony Price for page 103 middle right; Action Images for page 103 middle middle; Aspect Picture Library/John Walsh for page 103 middle left; Getty Images/Stewart Chen for page 36 bottom left, /Ken Fisher for page 36 top left, /David Higgins for page 36 top right, /Randy Wells for page 36 bottom right; Sally and Richard Greenhill for page 103 bottom left; Images Colour Library for page 103 top; D.Simson for page 123; Telegraph Colour Library/F.P.G./R Goldman for page 41 left, /V.C.L. for page 41 right

CONTENTS

PSST!

Introduction

To the trainees using *Tasks for Teacher Education*

Tasks for Teacher Education helps you to develop into an aware, self-critical teacher with a sense of self-direction. It contains a wide range of practical tasks which you experience as learners and teachers and is designed mainly for pre-service trainees and teachers of English as a foreign language and English as a second language. The tasks in the book may also be adapted for use by trainees and teachers of other foreign languages.

Our teaching and learning beliefs

Tasks for Teacher Education is based on a reflective model of teacher education, where you reflect both on your experiences as you do tasks and on your past experiences as a language learner and learn from them. You will not be told categorically how to teach. Instead, you will often be encouraged to evaluate a number of different options and then choose the one which most suits you and your situation.

Tasks for Teacher Education has been shaped by our own beliefs about teaching and learning, which we would like to share with you:

Learning-by-doing

By experiencing activities and discovering for yourself, you can learn more effectively. The tasks in *Tasks for Teacher Education* are experiential and help you discover aspects of teaching and learning for yourself.

Learning in groups

Working in groups is an effective way to learn about yourself and others. *Tasks for Teacher Education* encourages the group to value the knowledge, skills, needs, learning styles, personalities and interests each individual brings to the group.

Awareness

Awareness to us means understanding possible alternative directions to take and becoming more conscious of your own beliefs and attitudes about teaching and learning. In *Tasks for Teacher Education*, you are encouraged to develop awareness about teaching and yourself as a teacher.

Atmosphere

A group of learners who have good relationships with each other will learn better. In *Tasks for Teacher Education*, the creation of an effective, comfortable learning atmosphere is encouraged.

Existing experience and knowledge

Effective learning takes place when a trainer or teacher taps into the existing experience and knowledge of the learners in a group. *Tasks for Teacher Education* builds on your own rich classroom experiences, particularly as a language learner, to increase your learning as a teacher.

Individual responsibility

Ultimately, you are responsible for your own individual learning. As a teacher, you are alone in the classroom and your way of teaching is as unique as your fingerprint. Through using *Tasks for Teacher Education*, you will learn to take charge of your own professional life as a teacher. For the trainer, this means helping trainees to develop in areas they are interested in and to be more confident in choosing their own ways in becoming a teacher.

Alternatives

Just as there are always alternative ways to teach something, so can there be many different 'right ways' of teaching. *Tasks for Teacher Education* helps you to find your own preferred teaching style and to respond to your learners in your own way.

Key features of *Tasks for Teacher Education*

1 The Units

Each of the sixteen self-contained units deals with one topic and provides a variety of practical tasks. *Tasks for Teacher Education* is designed so that the units may be used separately and in any order. Each unit begins with a Map of the unit, which gives an overview of the whole unit and each separate task.

2 The Tasks

The tasks include:

- observation
- developing materials
- case studies
- role-plays
- simulations
- discussions
- readings
- brainstorming
- jigsaws
- evaluating tasks and techniques
- designing lesson plans
- matching
- microteaching
- journal entries
- games
- problem-solving
- questionnaires
- reflection
- ranking
- adapting materials
- mind maps
- classroom activity design
- homework

The tasks in *Tasks for Teacher Education* have been used by teachers and trainees in many different contexts and countries, from lengthy pre-service courses to weekend in-service sessions.

3 Further reading

At the end of each unit is an annotated list of suggested books or articles related to the unit topic, which will enable you to pursue points of particular interest or relevance to your own teaching situation and to develop your ideas further.

4 Glossary

The glossary of terms which follows this introduction, on pages viii-x, includes a list of defined terms which often occur in *Tasks for Teacher Education*.

5 Trainer's Book

The trainer's book for *Tasks for Teacher Education* contains trainer's notes and accompanying photocopiable material for use with the tasks. The photocopiable material is supplied as photocopy masters for ease of use. These masters include observation tasks, role cards, information-gap tasks, a lesson transcript, games and pictures.

More about the tasks

1 Observation tasks

Most units include Observation tasks; the teachers that you observe can be other trainees on teaching practice or experienced teachers. By using these observation tasks, you gain new insight into your *own* actions in the classroom. The areas of focus for observation vary (topics include, for example, *instruction giving, eliciting, dealing with spoken errors*), but each observation task requires you to watch a lesson closely and describe what you see. Your trainer will provide you with observation tables from the Photocopy Masters in the trainer's book to use while observing. After the observation task, post-observation questions guide you to reflect on what happened and to apply new ideas arising from the observation to your own teaching. **Unit 2 Mirror, Mirror on the Wall...** is an introduction to observation as a tool for teacher development.

2 Time out, take five: Journal entries

Most units of *Tasks for Teacher Education* contain Journal entries, within the section TIME OUT, TAKE FIVE. These assignments encourage you to pause for a few minutes and reflect and write about your own feelings and thoughts. Through writing in your journal, you develop your awareness of your own beliefs and attitudes. If you have never kept a journal before, concentrate on expressing your ideas in any way you can, reflecting on how you are developing. You might like to purchase a separate notebook to write in, as it is especially useful to re-visit journal entries and see how themes have reoccurred or your thoughts have changed over time. A few ways you can use journals include:

- writing to yourself: the contents of your journal are for your eyes only
- writing to a fellow trainee: write a dialogue in pairs, reacting to each other's journals
- writing to your trainer: establish a dialogue between you and your trainer around issues that are of concern to you[1]

3 Microteaching tasks

Microteaching tasks in *Tasks for Teacher Education* are denoted by the symbol **M** . During a microteaching task, one trainee teaches a short activity to fellow trainees for five or ten minutes.

[1] If you are interested in reading more about the use of journals in teacher education and teaching, read Porter et al, and Bailey in Richards and Nunan 1990.

The aims of these tasks are for you to experience teaching for a short time and to receive feedback in a supportive environment although the learning situation is inevitably a bit artificial and simplified. (It is unlikely, for example, that there will be discipline problems with a class of your peers.)

For each microteaching task, instructions are given for the trainee who is doing the microteaching: you will need to prepare in advance. Your trainer will provide you with any necessary material from the Photocopy Masters in the Trainer's Book. You then teach the short lesson and receive feedback.[2]

4 Feedback questions

After every microteaching task, there are Feedback questions which help you to focus on different aspects of teaching and to give appropriate feedback.

Giving feedback is probably the most important and exacting part of a microteaching task. After completing a microteaching task, it helps if sufficient time is saved for the trainee who taught to experience immediate feedback in order to ensure that the lesson is fresh in everyone's memory; alternatively, feedback can be given at a later stage.

It is vital that one's confidence in teaching is not shattered during a feedback session. To avoid this happening, after the very first microteaching session, you and your trainer can limit your feedback initially to only the positive elements. In later microteaching classes, you might discuss three positive points and three points for improvement (rather than three bad points!). It is essential always to include those positive parts – something positive can always be said about someone's teaching. It also helps perhaps to focus on a few elements only, rather than offer advice on many items at once, which might be overwhelming. If you do microteaching in pairs in initial microteaching activities, you can support each other both during preparation and feedback.

Some alternative ways of giving feedback after a microteaching task are:

- Give spoken and/or written feedback.
- Discuss what feedback to give in small groups and share each group's conclusions in class.
- Focus on only one aspect of teaching.
- Two or three trainees watch and complete an observation task; they do not participate in the activity. They then give feedback on what they observed.
- Appoint a secretary, who notes down what is said during the feedback session and gives the notes to the microteaching trainee after the discussion. These notes are then a concrete reminder about what was said during feedback.

5 Focus questions

In many of the tasks there are Focus questions which ask you to think about your learning and teaching. These give you an opportunity for reflection and consideration of your future teaching.

---

[2] To learn more about microteaching and its varieties, read Chapter 6, Microteaching, in Wallace 1992.

Symbols and abbreviations

Here are some recurrent symbols and abbreviations used throughout the book:

I individual task

P pair work

G small group work (3-5 participants)

C whole class task

M microteaching task

T   teacher

L   learner

Ls   learners

LA, LB learner A, learner B, etc.

L1, L2 first language, second language

CB   coursebook

**   error in English (placed next to an incorrect statement)

To avoid confusion, we have used the following terminology:

(teacher) trainer	the person who is leading teacher training classes
(teacher) trainee	participant on a course who is using this book
teacher	practising English language teacher
learner	secondary or primary pupil of English

For ease of reading, we have mostly used one personal pronoun, *she*. When needing to distinguish between two individuals, we have also used *he*. No sexism is intended.

Your feedback to us

We would very much like to hear your feedback on this book and any of the tasks, since we are continually updating our own ideas and tasks for teacher education. Write to us care of Longman:

Rosie Tanner and Catherine Green
Addison Wesley Longman
ELT Division
Edinburgh Gate
Harlow
Essex CM20 2JE
United Kingdom

GLOSSARY

This is an alphabetical list of terms which are used in *Tasks for Teacher Education.*

accuracy   The ability to produce language in an grammatically correct way. Compare *fluency.*

acquisition   See *language acquisition.*

activity   A short task which is part of a lesson, perhaps lasting 15-20 minutes. Synonymous here with *task.*

affective   Influencing or influenced by the emotions.

affective filter   An imaginary device, first used by linguist Stephen Krashen (1980) who believes that individuals with a positive attitude toward the target language and/or culture have a lower affective filter, a kind of screen through which new language and information passes on its way to the brain. According to Krashen, the lower the affective filter, the more language the individual is likely to acquire.

aims   The behavioural objectives of a lesson (e.g. *The learners will be able to order tickets for a film over the telephone.*)

authentic materials   Texts from real-life sources (e.g. magazine articles, original cassette recordings) originally intended for native speakers.

body language   Non-verbal communication. The way someone communicates a message with their body (e.g. by eye contact, facial expression, gestures, posture).

brainstorm   To collect together ideas very quickly, without judging whether the ideas are good or not. Also *a brainstorm.*

classroom management   The way a teacher organises her classroom and learners (e.g. how the furniture is organised, when to start and stop activities).

cloze   A technique used commonly in teaching reading and listening, where words are removed from a text and replaced by gaps. The learners then fill in the gaps.

communicative language teaching   The goal of this teaching method is communication, both in the classroom and in real life. It generally encourages more learner talk for real communicative purposes and a facilitative role for the teacher.

concept checking   In teaching vocabulary, a technique in which teachers check learners' comprehension of a new concept by asking related questions (e.g. What can you buy in a *bakery*?)

content-based   Focusing on a content area (e.g. the rain forest), so that learners will acquire language through a meaningful study of a content area.

dialogue journal   A written diary exchanged between two individuals (e.g. learner to learner, learner to teacher); content is more important than form. Errors are not addressed, generally.

EFL   Acronym for English as a Foreign Language. The role of English in a country where English is not a language of communication.

elicitation   A procedure where a teacher gets learners to produce language, draws information out of the learners. Also *to elicit* and *eliciting.*

error   A mistake made in language learning which shows that the learner hasn't yet learnt something. Compare *mistake.* See also page 93 for a dictionary definition.

evaluation   Gathering information about a class or an individual in order to form a judgement (e.g. about English level or about a trainee's teaching). Contrasted in this book with *observation.*

extensive reading   Reading a long text (e.g. a book) or a lot of text on a variety of topics to obtain an overall understanding of it. Compare *intensive reading.*

facilitator   An assistant to or a guide of a group, who helps the group to find their own answers rather than providing them with 'right' answers.

feedback   Information that is given to learners about their spoken or written performance, or to trainees or teachers about their teaching.

fluency   The ability to produce language easily, to communicate quickly but not necessarily with grammatical correctness. Compare *accuracy.*

genre   Type of text (e.g. a magazine, a letter, a note).

gist   The main idea or message of a text, either spoken or written.

group dynamics   The way a group of people interacts with each other.

humanistic activities   Teaching techniques which emphasise the whole person and acceptance of his or her individual values and emotions. Also *humanism*.

hyponym   A word which is included in the meaning of another word (e.g. *daisy* is a hyponym of *flower*). Compare *superordinate*.

inference   A guess about something from a text, reading between the lines. Also *to infer*.

information gap   An activity in which a learner knows something that another learner does not know, so has to communicate to 'close the gap'. Information gaps are used a lot in communicative language teaching (e.g. two learners have two different pictures and have to find the differences between them without showing their pictures to each other).

information transfer activity   An activity where a learner has to move information from one place to another (e.g. a learner has to complete a table according to information on a map).

input   Language which learners experience in a lesson, from which they can learn.

integrated skills   All of the language skills (listening, reading, speaking, writing) together. Integrated skills activities bring together different language skills (e.g. learners discuss a writing assignment, thus practising listening, speaking and writing).

intensive reading   Careful reading to obtain specific information from a text (usually a short text). Compare *extensive reading*.

interaction   Patterns of communication (verbal and non-verbal) between people.

jigsaw reading   An activity which involves re-ordering a mixed up text to find its correct order; it helps learners see the connections between parts of a written text.

journal   A written diary. Compare *dialogue journal*.

L1   The language you first know as a child.

L2   The language you learn second.

language acquisition   'Picking up' a language; not learning it consciously, but by being exposed to it in natural situations (e.g. as a child learns his first language). Often contrasted with *language learning*, which involves a conscious knowledge of the language (e.g. grammatical rules).

language skills   There are four principal language skills: listening, reading, speaking and writing. The skills also involve grammar and vocabulary.

learner-based activity   An activity in which learners supply personally relevant information (e.g. their favourite hobbies) or help create materials.

learner-centred teaching   Learning situations where information and ideas are brought to the class by learners and used as learning material and which are concerned with the interests, needs, learning styles, feelings, lives and/or values of learners.

learner talking time   The amount a learner (or learners) talk during a lesson.

learning strategy   A process or technique which a learner uses to help herself to learn a language (e.g. looking at a photograph above a newspaper article before reading is a reading strategy).

learning style   The way a particular learner learns something (e.g. by watching, by doing).

lexical set   A group of related words, a word family (e.g. a lexical set of furniture might be *chair*, *table*, *television*, *sofa*).

method   The procedures and techniques characteristic of teaching.

microteaching   A teaching situation which has been reduced in some way (e.g. the teacher's task is simplified, the lesson is very short, the class size is small); often used in a training situation to concentrate on one particular aspect of a trainee's teaching. Usually one trainee teaches a short activity to her classmates.

mind map   A diagram which supposedly represents the brain or the mind: topics are clustered on the page together as they are believed to be collected in the brain. For an example of a mind map, see page 43.

mistake   A mistake in linguistic terms is a language mistake made by a learner when he is careless. Compare *error*. See page 93 for a dictionary definition.

mixed-ability class   A group of learners whose proficiency levels span a range (e.g. high-beginning, low intermediate, high-intermediate).

monitoring   What a teacher does while learners are doing an activity (e.g. group work); walking around the class and listening to, checking or helping learners.

Monitoring is also used by linguists in connection with language learning theory; learners are considered to monitor their language when they are consciously following the (spoken or written) language they are producing.

observation   Gathering information together by watching a class, in order to describe what is happening. Contrasted in this book with *evaluation*.

perceptual learning style   A learning style related to the senses (e.g. an auditory learning style, a visual learning style). See **Unit 15: Us and Them** for tasks on perceptual learning styles.

personalisation   When learners communicate about themselves or their own lives.

pictogram   A drawing of a word which represents that word. See page 27 in **Unit 4: How Do You Do?** for an example.

pie chart   A circular graph, divided into sections like pie slices, useful for displaying the relationship of parts to each other and to the whole. See page 128 for an example.

post-listening
post-reading
post-speaking
post-writing   What is done after an activity, usually intended as a logical consequence to that activity (e.g. *post-reading* is done after reading).

pre-listening
pre-reading
pre-speaking
pre-writing   What is done before an activity to prepare learners for skills work (e.g. *pre-reading* is done before reading).

pre-teach   To prepare learners for an activity, by introducing new language or a topic.

problem-solving activity   An activity where a learner has to solve a problem (e.g. learners have descriptions of several applicants and have to decide together who might be the best one for a certain job).

productive skills   Speaking and writing. Learners are required to *produce* the language by speaking and writing. Compare *receptive skills*.

rank   To put items in a certain order, often in order of preference or importance.

realia   Things from real life which are used for learning (e.g. classroom furniture, pictures, household objects).

receptive skills   Listening and reading. Learners are *receiving* language and processing it, without producing it. Compare *productive skills*.

role-play   A communicative activity in which learners talk to each other in different character roles.

scanning   Reading quickly to find specific information from a text. Compare *skimming*.

simulation   A role-play where you play yourself in a given situation.

skills   See *language skills*.

skimming   Reading quickly to find the main idea(s) of a text. Compare *scanning*.

strategy   See *learning strategy*.

superordinate   A general term which includes other terms (e.g. *transport* is a superordinate). Compare *hyponym*.

synonym   A word which means the same, or nearly the same, as another (e.g. *large* is a synonym of *big*).

task   Another word for a short classroom activity.

tapescript   The transcription of a tape-recorded text, dialogue, etc.

teacher talking time   The amount of time a teacher talks in a lesson.

teaching space   The area that a teacher uses in the classroom while teaching.

time line   A straight line representing the passage of time, often used in teaching verb tenses.

transcript   A written record of what happens in a classroom.

transition   The way a teacher makes a link between two separate parts of a lesson.

while-listening
while-reading
while-speaking
while-writing   What learners do while they are doing another activity (e.g. a *while-listening* activity might be to tick boxes as learners are listening to a tape recording).

word set   See *lexical set*.

1 FIRST THINGS FIRST

The first lesson

Reflection

TASK 1 The first time ever I saw your face

In this task, you recall first lessons that you had and share your dreams and dreads about first lessons.

Step 1   **I**

Work individually.

Recall a first lesson or first lessons you had *as a learner*. It could be a first language lesson but it might equally be another type of lesson – a driving lesson, a sports lesson, a computing lesson, a drawing class. Think about the other learners, your feelings, your new teacher, your expectations, your fears, your first impressions of the subject. Write two lists: one of the positive aspects of your first lesson, the other of the negative aspects. Remember, think about yourself *as a learner*, not as a teacher.

Step 2   **G** and **I**

Work in groups.

1 Describe some of the positive and negative aspects of your first lesson in Step 1.

2 *a* As a learner, what do you ideally want to happen in a first lesson? In other words, what are your dreams for a first class? Individually, note down some dreams that you, *as a learner*, have for first lessons.

 b What do you dread in a first lesson? What do you *not* want to happen? Note down your dreads *as a learner*.

3 Share your wildest dream and your darkest dread with your group.

4 What kind of first impression would you, as a teacher, like to make on your learners? Share your ideas in your group.

Beliefs about first lessons

TASK 2 Digging deeper

In this task, you think about actions that teachers take in first lessons and the beliefs that might influence these actions.

Step 1   **P**

Work in pairs.

1 Look at the table below. On the left are actions that a teacher might take in a first lesson. On the right are beliefs which a teacher might have. Match each action with a belief or beliefs, by writing the letter(s) of the beliefs next to each action. There may be more than one answer for each. The first is done for you as an example.

2 Write any additional actions and beliefs of your own in the spaces provided.

3 Individually, circle the numbers of those actions that you would like to do in your own first lesson.

Step 2   **G**

Work in groups.

1 Discuss which actions and beliefs you matched.

2 Tell each other which actions you would take in your first lesson and why.

Actions in first lessons	Underlying beliefs
1 Establish a particular classroom atmosphere: co-operative and respectful. *Example:* *a i h*	*a* Learning means forming a series of good habits from the start.
2 Establish a code of classroom conduct (acceptable behaviour, etc.). _____	*b* Learners should understand what the course is about to be properly oriented and motivated to learn.
3 Learn about learners' expectations. _____	*c* Language is for communication, and learners should begin using a foreign language for this purpose.
4 Present the course: point out important information about course content, ways of working, assessment. _____	*d* Learners should take responsibility for their own learning.
5 Introduce yourself. _____	*e* A teacher must know something about her learners' personal lives to make the class interesting to them.
6 Learners introduce themselves, or each other, or learn something about each other. _____	*f* It is difficult and unnatural to work with strangers.
	g Learners' attitudes about the course will be formed quickly, by the end of the first lesson.
7 Pre-test learners to assess their proficiency level. _____	*h* A teacher cannot teach learners properly unless she knows who they are and what their needs are.
8 Teach a typical lesson, saving unusual activities (introductions, etc.) for the second lesson. _____	*i* Discipline is an important element in the classroom, and learners should be shown that early on.
	j Learning should be fun in order to be motivating.
	k Learners should believe that their teacher is well-qualified and interesting.
9 _____ _____	*l* _____
10 _____ _____	*m* _____
	n _____

Tasks for first lessons

TASK 3 Starting out

In this task, you evaluate different activities for first lessons.

Step 1 **G**

Work in groups.

Below and on pages 4-5 are six activities for first lessons; evaluate each of them by answering the Focus questions.

Focus questions

1 What is/are the aim(s) of the activity (it/they might be linguistic or other aims)?

2 What kind of class might do this activity (age, level, type of learner)?

3 What do you like about the activity?

4 What do you dislike about the activity?

5 Which activity out of the six would you prefer as a learner in a new class? Why?

6 Which activity out of the six would you prefer if you were the teacher of a new class? Why?

Activity A – Reverse role-play

1 Sit in pairs. Interview your partner for five minutes, remembering that in a few minutes you are going to role-play that person. You will have to answer questions about them as if you were them. Be prepared to answer as many questions as you can about them.

2 Change pairs and work with someone else in the class who you do not know. You now role-play the person you interviewed in (1). Work for five minutes and answer your new partner's questions as if you were that person. You might have to invent some responses but keep cool, be creative; if you get stuck, imagine what their answer(s) might be!

3 Return to your original partner. No doubt there will be some more questions that you need to ask them, to clarify some points or to discover some more information. Talk for five minutes and find out some more about them.

Activity B – Making rules

1 The teacher sets out three or four basic rules that she would like the class to keep, for example:

- please be on time for every class; I shall do the same

- homework must be handed in on time; I shall give you ample time to do it

- when I speak, please keep silent; when you speak, I shall also keep silent; (etc.)

2 The teacher invites the class to add any rules that they would like to be kept. Learners discuss their ideas in groups or give individual suggestions.

3 A poster is made and mounted (by the learners or the teacher) of the rules that the class has negotiated, so that everyone can see the rules.

Activity C – Names

You will need a large ball for this activity.

1 The whole class stands or sits in a circle. One person holds the ball. He throws the ball to someone else, shouting out his own name clearly. This continues until everyone has caught the ball and shouted out their own name.

2 The teacher then changes the activity: the person throwing the ball must name the person she is throwing to. This continues for a while.

3 Participants can throw the ball to someone whose name they have forgotten, asking, 'What's your name?' The person who catches the ball tells their name.

4 Continue the activity until everyone knows the names of most of their classmates.

Activity D – Questions first

1 Each learner thinks of one or two questions that they would really like to ask the other members of the class and writes them on a slip of paper. They can be about anything they choose.

2 All the class circulates to discover the answers to their own questions.

3 Hold a plenary where learners share interesting pieces of information with the whole class.

Activity E – Questionnaire

1 Divide the class into groups of about seven or eight. Each group has a few copies of the following questionnaire, enough for everyone to see a copy:

Ask everyone in your group the questions below. Put a tick (✔) in the YES column when someone answers *Yes* and a tick in the NO column when someone answers *No*.		
QUESTIONS	YES	NO
a Did you start learning English before you were seven? b Have you ever been to an English-speaking country? c Do you prefer speaking to writing in English? d Does one of your parents speak English? e Do you often write letters to someone in English? (etc.)		

2 Group members ask and answer the questions; they tick the appropriate column as many times as they get a YES or a NO answer.

3 The group then writes a short paragraph together about themselves, according to the information they gathered.

4 Each small group reads their paragraph to the whole class.

Activity F – Drawing my life

① On a blank sheet of paper, each class member draws five or six objects that they have used in the past few months and that illustrates something about them – their interests, recent events in their life, their family, etc. Reassure learners that they don't need to be good artists to do this: it might be more fun if they aren't.

② In pairs, As and Bs. A is silent, while B does some detective work, guessing what A's objects are and how they illustrate A's life. Only when B has exhausted his comments is A allowed to speak; A can then reveal some more information, or correct B's information.

③ Reverse roles: A becomes the detective and guesses about B's drawings. B then reveals whether the comments are true or not, and adds further information about himself.

④ The pairs can then introduce each other to the class.

Step 2

Work in pairs.

1 Read the brief descriptions of first English lessons (i) to (vii) in the box. Choose the activity from Step 1 which you think would be most appropriate for each first lesson (i) to (vii); write its letter in the right-hand column, or, if none is appropriate, suggest an entirely different activity.

First English lessons	Possible activity
(i) A group of twelve 10-year-olds who are new to English and new to you and each other.	
(ii) Thirty 12-year-olds who have had one year of English at various schools; only a few of them know each other.	
(iii) Your own first lesson in your first job. Your class is fifteen 15-year-olds who know each other well; it is their fourth year of English.	
(iv) A class of twenty-eight 13-year-olds who have a reputation for being noisy but friendly. They have been learning English and have been in the same class for two years; you have never taught them before.	
(v) A class of quite advanced learners who will be leaving school at the end of the term and who are taking an important English exam in two months' time. They know each other well.	
(vi) Twenty-eight adults; you taught them last year, which was their first year of English, and know them well.	
(vii) A group of intermediate-level 18-year-olds who are new to each other. They are false beginners who want to brush up their language skills in their spare time.	

Microteaching

TASK 4 First impressions

In this task, you design and teach an activity for a first lesson.

Step 1   **P**

Work in pairs.

1 Decide the type of first class you are going to teach. It might be:

- an imaginary class
- this first training class
- a real class.

2 Discuss the following factors about your class:

> - age of learners
> - motivation
> - level of English
> - number of learners
> - your familiarity with the learners
> - your own confidence with an activity
> - possible discipline problems
> - the learners' familiarity with each other
> - your learners' 'dreams and dreads'
> - the atmosphere you would like to create
> - length of the activity

3 Design a new activity or adapt one of the ideas in this unit for a first meeting with a class. It should last 5-10 minutes.

Step 2   **M**

1 One trainee teaches their activity to the class. If you are new to microteaching, read **3. Microteaching tasks** and **4. Feedback questions** on pages v-vi of the introduction.

2 Give feedback to each other on the effectiveness of the activity for a first lesson. Concentrate on giving positive feedback about the good elements of the lesson.

Time out, take five

Journal entry
My first class as a teacher trainee

Describe the first lesson of your teacher training course.

- What did the trainer do in your first class?
- Why do you think the trainer chose to act or teach as s/he did?
- What effect(s) did the trainer's actions in the first class have on you and the class?

2 MIRROR, MIRROR, ON THE WALL...

Classroom observation

Reflection

TASK 1 Picture this

In this task you reflect on how you feel about being observed.

Step 1   I

Work individually. Read the following situation.

Imagine you have been teaching English in a school for two months now. At the beginning of the week, the head of your school/director of studies tells you that she is going to observe your lessons during the next two weeks. Some days pass and now it is the evening before the observation.

Step 2   P

Work in pairs.

Make notes on your answers to the Focus questions.

Focus questions

1 How do you feel about being observed? (Think of two to six adjectives to describe your feelings.)

2 What expectations do you have of the person observing?

3 Why is the observer coming?

4 What will she look at?

5 How will the observer talk to you about the lesson (how soon afterwards, for how long, etc.)?

6 What kinds of topics might she touch on?

TASK 2 True confessions

In this task you read some opinions of experienced teachers about observation.

Step 1   I

Work individually.

Read the teachers' remarks about observation on page 8. Make notes on your answers to the following questions:

1 Whose opinion(s) do I agree with the most? Why?

2 Whose opinion(s) do I disagree with the most? Why?

Step 2   G

Discuss your opinions in groups.

In some ways I am not quite myself when I am being observed. I try to do my best and that means that I try to make sure both my English and my teaching are just perfect. I always hope that my learners will be on their best behaviour too, but you can't count on that.

— *Vanida*

I rarely have a chance to talk to other teachers about a new idea; we're all so busy. Recently, another teacher at my school asked me if I would like to come and observe some of her classes, and in exchange she would observe some of mine. At first I was a bit nervous, but then I thought, 'This is what I have been waiting for!' It's been one of the best things I've done and I definitely feel I have a buddy at work now.

— *Kinfe*

Maybe I'm weird, but I really like it when other teachers observe my classes. It's a good opportunity for me to get some feedback from a totally different perspective. Sometimes I invite another teacher to come and watch my class, and I ask her to observe a particular aspect of the lesson, such as trying to balance the class to get all the different levels of learners actively involved. It's so difficult teaching mixed-ability classes, and another teacher's feedback about what happened in my class is invaluable to me.

— *Anna*

I don't really mind when another teacher comes in to my class to observe my lesson. It's a great way to get new ideas about how to teach a particular point or handle a situation I usually find awkward or difficult. But I do feel as though our privacy is being invaded. I mean, I feel I have a certain rapport with my learners, and my classes have a positive atmosphere. When an outsider enters our classroom, there is always a chance that the special atmosphere we have created will be upset.

— *Tomek*

I dislike being observed. I feel like the person is judging me. It's usually the school inspector who observes my classes, and I feel he's only looking at what's wrong with my lesson. Maybe he's just trying to help me, but I resent his criticism. Why can't he spend an equal amount of time telling me about what is positive in my lessons?

— *Andreas*

Observing other teachers is something I began to do many years ago. At the very beginning I think I tended to be rather critical and constantly see the lesson in comparison to the way I think I'd teach it. But the more I did it, the better I became at it. Doing observations well is definitely something that takes some practice, but you can gain a lot from them, if you're willing to put in the effort.

— *Masaaki*

Observation vs. evaluation

TASK 3 Apples and oranges?

In this task you analyse the differences between observation and evaluation.

Step 1   **G**

Work in groups.

Discuss the Focus questions on page 9. As you answer, draw up a table comparing evaluation and observation (see example).

OBSERVATION	EVALUATION
1 describes an action or behaviour	1 judges an action or behaviour
2 focuses on one or many different acts or ways of behaviour	2 may be broad or narrow in focus, though general is more common
3 may be done by a teacher trainee, a fellow teacher, a parent or a school inspector	3 is usually done by a teacher's superior

Focus questions

1 What is the purpose of
a observation   **b** evaluation?

2 What is the focus of
a observation   **b** evaluation?

3 Who
a observes   **b** evaluates?

4 What forms are used by
a observers   **b** evaluators?

5 When is evaluation done?

6 When does a teacher see the observation form?

7 When do discussions take place following the observation?

Step 2

Work individually.

1 Read the passage **Reading: Observation and Evaluation** on page 11 in order to find additional differences between observation and evaluation.

2 Add any new information you find to your table.

Evaluating

TASK 4 Shifting viewpoints

In this activity you role-play a discussion between a teacher and an evaluator just after a lesson, then reflect on the experience.

Step 1   G

Work in groups.

1 Divide into four groups. Your trainer will give each group a different role card. Read the role card for your group and then examine the lesson you hear, watch or read about. As you experience the lesson, stay in role.

Your role cards are:
   Group 1 Role 1: Enthusiastic teacher
   Group 2 Role 2: Critical teacher
   Group 3 Role 3: Supportive evaluator
   Group 4 Role 4: Negative evaluator

2 Do one of three things, as directed by your trainer:
a Listen to a recording of a lesson, *or*
b Read a transcript of a lesson, *or*
c Watch a lesson on video.

3 During and after the lesson, take notes on your experience: list 'positive' comments and 'negative' comments. Remember: write in role!

Step 2   P

Work in pairs.

Pair up with another person so that one teacher and one evaluator are working together. Role-play a short discussion about the lesson, remembering to stay in role as you talk to each other.

Step 3   G

Work in groups.

Create new groups of four: each group should contain, as far as possible, someone from the original groups 1, 2, 3 and 4. Complete the statements and discuss the following questions:

1 As a teacher, I felt ... during the role-play with the evaluator because...

2 As an evaluator, I felt ... during the role-play with the teacher because...

3 Personally, did you agree with the person whose role you played?

4 What is your real, personal evaluation of the lesson?

5 How did you feel if your own evaluation of the lesson was quite different from that of the role you played?

Step 4   C

Work as a whole class.

Discuss the following Focus questions.

Focus questions

1 Is an evaluation usually negative? How could it be different?

2 What effect on the teacher might an evaluator's words have?

3 What cultural rules of behaviour exist in your teaching situation which may influence a face-to-face meeting between teacher and evaluator?

4 How might an evaluator's particular interest or point of view influence his impression of the lesson?

5 When is a good time to schedule a discussion about a lesson? Why?

Observing

TASK 5 Excuse me, may I come in?

In this task you reflect on how to approach a teacher whose class you wish to observe.

Step 1   G

Work in groups.

1 Brainstorm the most important things you think you should mention to a teacher whose lesson you are going to observe. Make a 'What?' list. For example:

> ### What?
> - who I am (name/school/position)
> - when I want to visit

2 For each point you list, note the reason for your idea in a 'Why?' list. For example:

> ### Why?
> - identify myself to T
> - clarify date, timetable conflicts

Step 2   C

Share your answers with the class.

TASK 6 Telescopic or microscopic viewing?

In this task you experience and analyse two different kinds of observation tables.

Step 1   P

Work in pairs.

Your trainer will give you a **Class observation table**, A or B. Observe a lesson, using one of the two tables.

Step 2   G

Work in groups.

1 Read each other's observation tasks.

2 Discuss the following Focus questions.

Focus questions

a What was the purpose of each observation?

b How easy was it to use the observation task?

c How accurately does each observation task describe or record what happens in the classroom?

d Which sample, A or B, do you prefer? Why?

3 Complete a table like the one below based on your discussion of the above questions.

Telescopic or microscopic viewing?

PROS (Reasons For)	CONS (Reasons Against)
Table A	Table A
Table B	Table B

Time out, take five

Journal entry
Nerves of steel

How confident do you feel about observing?

How have your ideas about observation changed since you first read the title of this unit?

How confident do you feel about making observations?

What do you think you, personally, can learn from observing?

Reading: Observation and Evaluation
(for **Task 3 Apples and Oranges?**, p.8)

As your class discussion may have pointed out already, *observation* may be very broad and cover a variety of issues, or it may be extremely narrow and focus on only one aspect of the classroom experience. More and more, teacher trainees, current teachers, teacher trainers, researchers and even school inspectors are making observations in order to *learn* something about the classroom experience while it is happening. They do not necessarily watch in order to judge whether the lesson is good or bad, but rather to describe what is happening. The point of their observations is to provide a kind of mirror for themselves or the person doing the teaching; the mirror may help the observed or the observer to see the action that takes place in the classroom more clearly.

The ultimate aim of *observing*, then, is to learn more about what teaching and learning are about: an observer may focus, for example, on a teacher's eye contact with her learners and discover that she is not looking at everyone during the lesson. The observer may decide that he, as a teacher, will consciously try to sweep his eyes over his own class (now or in the future) and make eye contact with all the learners. On the other hand, by focusing on a particular point, the observer may discover that he already behaves in a similar way to this teacher or in a different way from her. In both cases the observer develops an awareness of a behaviour found in the classroom, and this awareness can be useful in generating alternative actions or changes that might be appropriate in another classroom situation.

Evaluation, on the other hand, means that someone is placing value on some behaviour, either an act of the teacher or the learners. The evaluator may be trying to decide how good the teacher is, or how well the learners are progressing, for example. A written record may be put into the teacher's file and used later to help determine how the teacher is progressing in her work.

To conclude, in this book in general and in this unit in particular, observation is seen as a learning tool and thus is not used in order to pass judgement on someone's teaching practices.

Further reading

Allwright, Dick. 1988. *Observation in the Language Classroom.* Harlow: Addison Wesley Longman.
   An account of classroom observation from an historical and educational perspective.

Bowers, Roger (Ed.). 1987. *Language Teacher Education: An Integrated Programme for ELT Teacher Training (ELT Documents: 125).* London: Modern English Publications and The British Council.
   Contains an appendix of 10 worksheets with instructions for use in classroom observation.

Day, Richard. 1990. 'Teacher Observation in Second Language Teacher Education' in Richards, J. C. and D. Nunan (Eds.), *Second Language Teacher Education.* Cambridge: Cambridge University Press, pp. 43-61.
   Explains the advantages and disadvantages of several techniques and instruments for observation.

Fanselow, John. 1987. *Breaking Rules: Generating and Exploring Alternatives in Language Teaching.* New York: Addison Wesley Longman.
   Helps teachers look at what happens in the classroom and think about new or different ways of doing things.

Hancock, Robert and David Settle. 1990. *Teacher Appraisal and Self-Evaluation.* Oxford: Basil Blackwell.
   Practical activities to promote self-evaluation.

Malamah-Thomas, Ann. 1987. *Classroom Interaction.* Oxford: Oxford University Press.
   Contains 155 tasks on the topic of classroom interaction. Many of the activities are well suited for observation tasks.

Nunan, David. 1989. *Understanding Language Classrooms: A Guide for Teacher-Initiated Action.* Hemel Hempstead: Prentice-Hall International.
   Contains a range of observation tasks, from easy-to-use to fairly complex.

Wallace, Mike. 1991. *Training Foreign Language Teachers: A Reflective Approach.* Cambridge: Cambridge University Press.
   Chapter 5 and Chapter 7 provide a discussion of central issues in observation as well as several useful observation tasks.

Wajnryb, Ruth. 1992. *Classroom Observation Tasks: A Resource Book for Language Teachers and Trainers.* Cambridge: Cambridge University Press.
   This book includes 35 observation tasks in seven different areas. Each task includes a guide for preparation for and follow-up to the observations.

3 GRASPING GRAMMAR

Presenting structures

Reflection

TASK 1 What's grammar got to do with it?

In this task, you reflect on your own beliefs about
the role of grammar in learning English.

Step 1 **I**

Work individually.

1 Read the two statements below about learning
and teaching grammar and decide to what extent
you agree or disagree with each one:

> You don't really need to teach grammar explicitly,
> saying things like, 'This is the past perfect tense
> and you form it like this'. That's unnecessary.
> Learners will pick it up for themselves. If they
> want grammar, the teacher can give them exercises
> to do outside class, but don't waste precious class
> time teaching it. I think it's better to teach
> learners to communicate, to practise as much
> English as possible in class with real language.
> Grammar will look after itself.

Amanda

> I always look over a new unit in a book and then
> teach my pupils the grammar rule before we even
> begin the unit; I explain the rules that are going
> to come up and then do some exercises with the
> class. That really helps them to be clear about
> what the unit is about and they can do the
> activities in the unit better. I think they learn
> better that way.

Julio

2 Now write a short paragraph about your own
beliefs about the role of grammar in English lessons.

Step 2 **C**

Discuss some of your ideas with your class.

Microteaching

TASK 2 Making connections

In this task, you think about effective grammar presentation techniques and then present a new grammar point to your class. If you are new to microteaching, read **3. Microteaching tasks** and **4. Feedback questions** on pages v-vi of the introduction.

Step 1

Work in groups.

Make a list of what you think are effective grammar presentation techniques. For example:

<u>Effective Grammar Presentation Techniques</u>

- Use visual aids to help students memorise something.

- State the aims of a presentation so learners know what is coming later.

Step 2   **I**

Work individually.

You are going to present a new grammar point to a group of three or four classmates. Choose one of the following:

- the use of *much* and *many*
- the difference between the simple present tense and the present continuous tense
- imperatives
- present tense of the verb *to be*
- past tense questions
- other (your own choice).

Your lesson must last *only ten minutes*, so do not be over-ambitious. As you prepare your mini-lesson, think about:

- the exact aims of your presentation
- effective presentation techniques
- stages in your presentation

- how much time you will need for each stage
- materials (e.g. visuals, the blackboard, realia)
- how you might involve your group.

Step 3   and **G**

1 Appoint a timekeeper.

2 Each person has ten minutes to present their grammar point. The timekeeper must watch the time strictly: even if the lesson is not finished, tell the teacher to stop after ten minutes.

3 Again, strictly limiting yourselves to ten minutes, discuss your answers to the Feedback questions below.

Feedback questions

a What was clear about the grammar presentation?

b What might be added to clarify it further?

c What might have been changed to make the learning more effective?

d What was particularly effective about the teaching?

e Any other comments?

4 The next person presents their grammar point and receives feedback.

Presenting

TASK 3 Let me count the ways...

In this task, you evaluate twelve presentation techniques for the present perfect tense.

Step 1   **P**

Work in pairs.

Read each of the techniques on pages 16-19 for presenting the present perfect tense to a class for the first time. Then complete the table opposite. In the appropriate columns, make notes on the advantages and possible problems of each technique. One example is done for you.

Grammar presentation techniques		
Technique	**Advantages**	**Possible problems**
1 Using a song text		
2 Using a time line		
3 Reading		
4 Using a picture		
5 Using realia		
6 Personalising		
7 Explaining directly		
8 Practising and presenting	- uses Ls' real lives; - clear explanation given - Ls begin with the use, then learn the form - some amusing questions	- Ls might not understand the questions - needs good elicitation techniques from T - Ls have to be used to working in pairs - not much context provided
9 Discovering		
10 Using a chart		
11 Eliciting		
12 Comparing L1 and L2		

PRESENTATION TECHNIQUES

1 USING A SONG TEXT

The teacher finds a song text which contains a lot of present perfect tenses. She makes a worksheet where some of the present perfect tenses are pasted out and, as the learners listen to the song on the cassette recorder, they try to fill in the gaps. She then asks for the answers, and asks the learners why the present perfect tense is used and not the past tense. She gradually elicits (or explains, if necessary) the use and form of the present perfect tense.

2 USING A TIME LINE

The teacher draws a time line on the board, representing the example sentence *I have seen her* as the dotted line I- - - - - - - - -I on the diagram below. She tells her class that it is placed between PAST and NOW because it represents the present perfect used for unspecified time: I saw her, but I don't tell you when or where so I use the present perfect tense.

I have seen her
|- - - - - - -|
PAST ——————— NOW ——————— FUTURE

3 READING

Learners do the following worksheet in groups:

Here is part of Ursula's school report.

SCHOOL REPORT

FIELDMORE SCHOOL   Winter term

Name: Ursula Jones   **Age:** 12   **Class:** 1G

Subject	Mark	Remarks
ENGLISH	A	Very good. Ursula has worked hard this term and has received high marks in her tests. Well done! P.B.
GEOGRAPHY	C	An average mark this term. Ursula likes Geography but has found it difficult this term. She has written an interesting project about the Lake District. H.T.
MATHS	B	Ursula has had a good term; she has worked very hard and has improved a lot. Keep it up! J.O.
SPORT	B	Ursula has enjoyed her dance classes this term and has done very well. She has also done well in gymnastics. P.W.

Read Ursula's report. Are these sentences true (T) or false (F)?

1 Ursula has worked hard in Geography. T/F
2 She has received low marks in her English test. T/F
3 She has written a project about Wales. T/F
4 She has not worked hard in her Maths lessons. T/F
5 She has danced in the Sports lessons. T/F
6 She has done better in Maths this term than she did last term. T/F

Now write two more sentences about Ursula:

7 She has _____.

8 She has _____.

4 USING A PICTURE

The teacher shows the learners pictures A and B below.

The teacher explains that picture B is now and picture A was at 7 o'clock this morning. She makes statements pointing out the differences between the pictures, such as, *In picture B, the children have come to school*. She asks the class to try to make some sentences for themselves in pairs; learners try to make sentences. The teacher elicits their sentences and corrects their mistakes. (Learners are unlikely to make well-formed sentences at this stage because they have never encountered the tense formally before although they are likely to recognise it.)

The teacher asks the learners to repeat some of the sentences that were made during the presentation and writes them on the board. She points out how to form the present perfect tense and explains that it is used when we are talking about events that happened in the past but we don't know exactly when.

5 USING REALIA

The teacher puts some objects on a desk in front of the class: her briefcase, some books, her cup of coffee, her chalk, and some objects from the learners in her class. She then asks the class to close their eyes or turn around for a few seconds, and quickly moves some objects. She asks the class, *What have I moved?* and tries to elicit examples of the present perfect using *You have moved* from them. For example, *You have moved the coffee, You have moved the blue book*. She writes examples of the sentences that she or the learners have provided on the board.

6 PERSONALISING

The teacher writes the names of five people she knows on the board. She tells the class about each of the five people, using a present perfect tense with *just* for each one, for example, *My son has just started school* or *My friend Yuri has just gone to Greece on holiday*. She writes the sentences on the board, explaining that if we use *just* and the present perfect tense, and we don't say exactly when, it means that something has happened in the very recent past.

She explains the third person form of the present perfect tense (*has* plus the past participle) and asks the learners to write down the names of five people they know. The learners then try to use the present perfect tense, writing about the five people in their lives, using the present perfect and *just*.

7 EXPLAINING DIRECTLY

The teacher writes the form of the present perfect on the board and explains to the class that the present perfect is used:

(i) for unspecified time in the past and

(ii) when something started in the past and is still true now.

She gives some examples to illustrate, for (i) *I have been to America* and for (ii) *She has lived here for five years*.

8 PRACTISING AND PRESENTING

The teacher gives out the table below, asking learners to work in pairs and to ask and answer the questions. The learners are familiar with the vocabulary in the table, but not with the present perfect tense. She does a few examples with individual learners first.

Have you ever seen	an elephant? your great-grandmother or great-grandfather? a television programme about dolphins? a UFO or a spaceship? a shooting star? the Mediterranean Sea? the Tower of London? (etc.)	No, I haven't. Yes, I have.

The teacher gradually elicits the form of present perfect tense questions by asking her class, *What question did I ask you?* Some learners will probably reproduce her question, with prompting. She eventually writes on the blackboard:

Present Perfect Tense Questions

has/have + person + past participle?
(Have)   (you)   (seen)

She asks the class when they think these types of questions are used. The learners explain to the teacher what they think. She explains that the present perfect tense is used with *Have you ever...?* to ask general questions about what people have done in the unspecified past.

9 DISCOVERING

The teacher asks the learners to look at a reading passage which the learners have studied before as a reading text. The learners then guess in groups which of the following sentences (a) to (g) are *grammatically* correct (C) or incorrect (I) and circle the C or the I next to each sentence:

(a) The children have brought pencils to the lesson.   C / I
(b) The children has understand Miss Honey's speech about Mrs Trunchbull.   C / I
(c) Matilda have begun school a bit late.   C / I
(d) The children have just start school.   C / I
(e) The lessons has started today.   C / I
(f) Matilda has not been to school before.   C / I
(g) Miss Trunchbull has been Headmistress for a long time.   C / I

Learners then complete the two substitution tables below. If they have problems, the teacher supplies them with the words *have* and *has*, but does not tell the learners where to place the words until they have tried for themselves.

THE PRESENT PERFECT: STATEMENTS

Subject	have/has	Rest of sentence
I, you, we, they, the children		_____ school.
he, she, (it), Matilda		

After the learners have completed the table, the teacher asks them to correct the original incorrect sentences (a) to (g). She checks their answers.

10 USING A CHART

The teacher draws the following chart on the board:

Name	France	Spain	India	Britain	USA
Rudi		✓		✓	
Liu Feng				✓	✓

She asks different learners in the class, *Have you been to France?* or *Have you been to India?*, completing the table by ticking (✓) the appropriate boxes as the learners give their answers. Once the chart is complete with, say, five learners, she asks the class what question she was asking. She then writes her question on the board and gives a short explanation of the form of the present perfect tense and its question form. She rubs the ticks off the board. Learners then copy the empty table into their notebooks, leaving space for five names and ticks. They then ask each other the question *Have you been to...?* and tick the appropriate boxes in their tables. Afterwards, they write five sentences in their notebooks about the five people they interviewed (for example, *Rudi has been to Spain and Britain*).

11 ELICITING

The teacher tells her class what she has done this morning: *I've had my breakfast. I've said goodbye to my children. I've drunk two cups of coffee. I've driven to school.* (etc.) She writes on the board, *What have you done this morning?* and then asks individual learners this question, gradually eliciting present perfect sentences from her learners. If they make mistakes, she corrects them gently. She slowly builds up correct present perfect sentences on the board (*I've fed my dog, I've eaten some bread*) and also writes up some non-contracted forms (*I have fed my dog,* etc.) She then points out that the present perfect tense is used for unspecified past time – if the time in the past when an event happened is *not* mentioned, the present perfect tense is often used.

12 COMPARING L1 AND L2

A French-speaking teacher of English introduces the present perfect tense, pointing out the differences between the use and the form of the present perfect tense in English and the perfect and past tenses in French.

Step 2

Work in pairs.

1 If you were introducing the present perfect tense for the first time, which of the twelve presentation techniques would you use? (You may choose to combine several of them.)

2 In which order would you use your chosen presentation techniques?

3 Share your answers with your class and the reasons for your choice(s).

TASK 4 Getting it across **P**

This task focuses on presenting both the form and the use of a new grammar point.

1 Read the passage opposite, **Form and Use**, and then do the task in pairs.

2 In the twelve presentations in **Task 3: Let me count the ways...**, the form and the use were both presented. But which use of the present perfect tense was presented in each one?

Complete the table below with the use of the present perfect which was presented in each case. Two examples are done for you.

Form and Use

When we present a new grammar point to learners, it is useful to present two different aspects: its form and its use.

Form means the grammatical form of an item and the rules for it. For example, does a word have an *s* at the end? When do we add an *-ed* to the end of a verb and when not? What is the word order of a question? When do you use *do* and when do you use *did* in a question?

Use deals with context. When or where is an item used? To discover the use of an item, ask yourself, *In which situation is an item used in natural communication?* For example, one use of the present simple tense is for describing actions that people do every day (*I get up at 7.30*), so in your presentation for the present simple tense you might include a natural situation where a person is telling someone else what they do every day, such as a learner writing to a new penfriend, telling her about a typical day at his school.

Technique	Which use of the present perfect is presented?
1 Using a song text	
2 Using a time line	*unspecified time in the past*
3 Reading	
4 Using a picture	
5 Using realia	
6 Personalising	
7 Explaining directly	
8 Practising and presenting	*questions and tag questions; general questions in the past with <u>ever</u>*
9 Discovering	
10 Using a chart	
11 Eliciting	
12 Comparing L1 and L2	

TASK 5 Jumbled grammar

In this task, you re-organise a mixed-up grammar presentation and evaluate it.

Step 1   **P**

Work in pairs.

Your trainer will give you a copy of a jumbled lesson plan which is a presentation of *Would you like to...?*[1] Organise the lesson plan into a logical order. The lesson plan begins with (m) and ends with (f).

Eliciting and observation

TASK 6 Drawing it out

In this task, you observe eliciting techniques.

Step 1   **I**

Work individually.

Arrange to observe a teacher or, if possible, more than one teacher to obtain different styles of eliciting. Read through this entire task before you begin. Your trainer will give you a copy of the **Observation table: Eliciting** to record at least *five times* when eliciting takes place in the class(es) you observe.

Step 2   **I**

Work individually.

Answer the Post-observation questions individually in writing as soon as possible after you have done the observation task.

Post-observation questions

1 Which eliciting techniques did the teacher use?

a face (e.g. questioning look)
b words (e.g. question words)
c body language (e.g. gestures with hands)
d intonation
e questions
f other

[1] This lesson is based on Unit 21, *Mode 1.*

Step 2   **P** and **C**

Work in pairs and answer the Focus questions below.

Focus questions

1 *a* Which of the presentation techniques in **Task 3 Let me count the ways...** were used in the grammar presentation?
b Why do you think the presentation techniques were used in this particular order?

2 Which other presentation techniques were used?

3 Think of *one* other presentation technique which could have been used in this presentation and add another stage to the middle of the lesson. Share your ideas with your class.

2 How did the teacher use silence while waiting for responses? (For example, the teacher waited a few seconds for a learner's response, but not long enough for the learner to become embarrassed.)

3 How did the teacher indicate that the learners had right answers?

4 How did the teacher indicate that the learners had wrong answers?

Step 3   **G**

Work in groups.

Discuss the eliciting that you observed in class and then together write a list of what you think are effective eliciting techniques (e.g. What were the best types of eliciting you observed? Which question words (who/what, etc.) were most effective in eliciting responses from learners? What successful use of body language or visuals did you observe?).

Example

Effective Eliciting Techniques

- use a lot of body language
- rephrase questions so Ls have more than one chance to answer

TASK 7 The eliciting game   **G**

This is a game where you practise your eliciting skills. Your trainer will provide the eliciting cards.

Materials per group

- one set of **Eliciting Cards**
- a watch with a second hand

Rules

1 Work in groups of four to six. Place the cards, face down, in the middle of your group. Appoint one person as a timekeeper.

2 The first player takes the top card, without saying what is on it. He must elicit what is on the card from the rest of the group in two minutes. He is allowed to use gestures, paper and pen – in fact, any resources he can think of. If he manages to elicit what is on his card, he can keep the card. If not, or if he accidentally reveals what is on the card, the card is replaced at the bottom of the pile.

Example:

Four players sit around a table. Player 1 picks a card which says 'six examples of sentences with *is*'. She says, *Tell me something about Han* and the group starts telling her. Each time she elicits a sentence containing *is*, she writes it on a piece of paper on the table in front of the group, encouraging the group to create sentences particularly with *is*, perhaps asking further questions, such as, *Is he old?* or *Is he a teacher?* until she has elicited six sentences.

3 Player 2 repeats the process.

4 The winner is the player with the most cards at the end.

....

Further reading

Carlisi, Karen and Jocelyn Steer. 1991. *The Advanced Grammar Book*. Boston, Massachusetts: Heinle and Heinle.
  A communicatively-oriented grammar textbook for advanced learners.

Celce-Murcia, Marianne and Diane Larsen-Freeman. 1983. *The Grammar Book: An ESL/EFL Teacher's Course*. Boston, Massachusetts: Heinle and Heinle.
  An exhaustive review of English grammar, with insights into the everyday needs of teachers.

Frank, Christine and Mario Rinvolucri. 1983. *Grammar In Action*. Oxford: Pergamon.
  Fun awareness activities for grammar learning for elementary and intermediate learners.

Harmer, Jeremy. 1987. *Teaching and Learning Grammar*. Harlow: Addison Wesley Longman.
  Practical suggestions for grammar teaching.

Rinvolucri, Mario. 1984. *Grammar Games* and Rinvolucri, Mario. 1995. *More Grammar Games*. Cambridge: Cambridge University Press.
  Games for practising grammar.

Quirk, Randolph and Sidney Greenbaum. 1973. *A University Grammar of English*. Harlow: Addison Wesley Longman.
  A very complete grammar reference.

Ur, Penny. 1988. *Grammar Practice Activities*. Cambridge: Cambridge University Press.
  As the title suggests, a mixture of interesting activities for practising grammar.

Willis, Dave. 1991. *Collins Cobuild Student's Grammar*. London: HarperCollins.
  Grammar explanations and exercises, with examples taken from the COBUILD Database of authentic English.

4 HOW DO YOU DO?

Introducing vocabulary

MAP OF UNIT

Reflection

TASK 1 At first sight

In this task you consider how to present vocabulary to make learning effective.

Step 1

Work individually.

1 Write down five or more words or phrases that you have recently learnt while studying a foreign language or that you remember learning in a particular situation in the past. 'Learnt' means really learnt and remembered, so that they are words which have remained in your memory.

2 Write down the reasons why you learnt those particular words, and perhaps not others which were presented to you. What made the experience memorable and effective?

Examples:

BRIEFCASE

> The teacher showed us her briefcase and we learnt what it was called: actually seeing and touching that green briefcase helped me remember its name.
>
> — *Erkan*

JUS

> I remember sitting in a café in Amsterdam and a friend ordering me an orange juice, which in Dutch is 'jus'; I remember I found it strange that the Dutch use a French word, but perhaps because of that I remember learning the word 'jus' on that particular day.
>
> — *Rosie*

SHAVE, SHOWER, BRUSH MY TEETH

> The teacher made me laugh because he mimed the presentation of some verbs (shave, shower, brush my teeth): because of that mime, I remembered the words.
>
> — *Samuel*

Step 2   **G**

Work in groups.

1 Share two words or phrases that you each learnt and discuss your reasons for learning them.

2 Now relate your vocabulary learning experiences to presenting new words or phrases in the classroom. Together, make a list of ten elements which constitute for you an *effective presentation* of

new vocabulary: what, in other words, in the classroom, makes something new really stick?

Example:

Effective presentation techniques

1. Using real things
    (as in <u>briefcase</u> example)

Presenting vocabulary

TASK 2 Mark my words

In this task, you evaluate different ways of presenting vocabulary.

Step 1   **P**

Work in pairs.

Spread over the following pages are eleven different techniques for presenting new vocabulary. Spend about ten minutes looking quickly at all the techniques and answering the Focus questions.

Focus questions

1 Which *four* techniques do you personally prefer? Why?

2 Which *one* technique would make the words 'stick' best? Why?

3 Which *one* technique do you consider the least effective? Why?

4 Which techniques were commonly used when you were first learning a foreign language?

5 Which techniques do you think are especially popular in your teaching situation now?

6 What other techniques do you know for presenting new vocabulary?

1 Realia and visuals

Show real objects or pictures of real objects to your learners.

Example:

> The topic of a unit is cooking. The teacher brings the following kitchen tools into class and shows them to the learners:
>
> bowl   whisk   fork   spoon   knife
> wooden spoon
>
> She then cooks something, using the items and repeating the new words often.

2 Word-building

Use parts of words to help learners build words or guess their meaning.

Example:

> # **Vocabulary Development**
>
> **Prefixes**
>
> **We can change the meaning of an adjective by putting a prefix in front of it. Add the prefix *un—*, *in—* or *im—* to these adjectives and put them in the correct column. Check in your dictionary to see if you put *un—* or *in—*. You put *im—* in front of most adjectives beginning with *m* or *p*.**
>
> | | | | | |
> |---|---|---|---|---|
> | tidy | dependent | safe | exciting | mature |
> | happy | precise | adequate | polite | patient |
> | friendly | expensive | interesting | competent | |
> | realistic | possible | human | perfect | |

Taken from Mode 2

3 Matching

Learners match words to words (e.g. synonyms or opposites) or sentences (e.g. definitions) or pictures.

Examples:

Find these nouns in the text. Match them with the definitions.

1	ghetto blaster	—	a large piece of material with a message written on it
2	raids	*1*	a radio-cassette player with built-in speakers
3	broadcasting	—	surprise attacks
4	resurgence	—	a tax on the reproduction of music for the public
5	airwaves	—	commerce
6	following	—	the means by which radio signals are transmitted
7	banner	—	supporters
8	copyright levies	—	reappearance and growth
9	trade	—	transmission of radio or television programmes

Taken from *Mode 3*

---

5 Song *The Monster Rock*

a 🔲 *Listen to the song and match the words on the left with the words on the right. Then match them with the correct pictures.*

clap		arms
shake		feet
snap	your	toes
stamp		hands
swing		head
wiggle		fingers

Taken from *Mosaic 1*

4 Guessing from context

Use the context surrounding a word to guess its meaning.

Example:

Yesterday's weather

Worldwide

(Temperatures at midday yesterday)

		°C	°F				°C	°F
Amsterdam	F	35	95	Istanbul	S		24	75
Athens	S	28	82	London	F		18	64
Berlin	F	18	64	Madrid	S		32	90
Birmingham	C	15	59	Manchester	C		12	54
Bombay	F	33	91	Moscow	C		19	66
Brussels	F	15	59	Newcastle	C		15	59
Buenos Aires	C	12	54	Paris	F		17	63
Cairo	F	32	90	Perth	C		11	52
Chicago	S	30	86	Rome	S		23	73
Dublin	F	15	59	Sydney	C		17	63
Edinburgh	R	14	57	Washington	S		27	81
Glasgow	R	14	57	Wellington	S		10	50

°C = degrees Centigrade   °F = degrees Fahrenheit

C = Cloudy F = Fair R = Rain S = Sunny

London readings

From 6 pm Friday to 6 am Saturday: Min temp ... °C (37°F). From 6 am to 6 pm Saturday: Max

5 Look at the weather report. What do these words mean?

worldwide	temperature	degrees
Centigrade	Fahrenheit	

Taken from
Fountain Elementary

5 Demonstrating

Act out, mime or demonstrate words.

Example:

The class is going to listen to a song, where they have to act out these verbs:

clap   shake   snap   stamp   swing   wiggle

As an introduction, the teacher acts out the words and asks the class to act, too.
As the words occur in the song, the learners act out the words.

6 Synonyms

Use words learners already know to teach them similar words.

Example:

Learners read a text and have to find the words in the text which mean the following:

very thin	*identical*
short and fat	*tiny*
very large	*crying*

7 Familiar or famous words

Use well-known English song titles, books or people.

Example:

> When introducing new words, the teacher reminds learners of famous or familiar places where they might have come across the words before, for example in film titles or songs or pop groups.
>
> Examples:
>
> wiggle   pop song with chorus 'Wiggle, wiggle'
>
> jungle   *Jungle Book*
>
> rolling   The Rolling Stones

8 Examples

Give examples of words you want to introduce.

Example:

> The teacher wants to introduce the word *fruit*. She explains that you can eat fruit and there are various kinds: apples, bananas, peaches, oranges, etc. (The class knows the words for some individual fruits already.) She asks the learners for more examples of fruit.

9 Pictograms

Draw the words to represent their meaning.

Example:

> ### 1 Vocabulary
>
> **a** *Look at the adjectives below. Match the opposites.*
>
> **b** *Name two things for each adjective.*
>
> *hot – the sun, a cup of coffee*
>
> **c** *How many more adjectives do you know? Write a list.*
>
> **d** *Draw two of these adjectives. Give them to a friend. Can he or she say what they are and draw their opposites?*

Taken from *Mosaic 2*

10 Translating

Translate words into L1.

Example:

> **Find these words in the text and decide if they are nouns (*n*), verbs (*v*) or adjectives (*adj*).**
>
> | | |
> |---|---|
> | earth ____ _____ | spades ____ _____ |
> | hailed ____ _____ | milestone ____ _____ |
> | adjourned ____ _____ | inquiry ____ _____ |
> | cruelty ____ _____ | foxhole ____ _____ |
> | buried ____ _____ | lungs ____ _____ |
> | savaged ____ _____ | injuries ____ _____ |
> | denied ____ _____ | cage ____ _____ |
> | captive ____ _____ | soil ____ _____ |
> | provide ____ _____ | wound ____ _____ |
> | badger-baiting ____ _____ | tied ____ _____ |
> | abused ____ _____ | |
>
> **Work out their meaning from the context and write a translation.**
> **Discuss your translations with another student and change as necessary. Now check your answers with your teacher or in a dictionary.**

Taken from *Mode 3*

11 Dictionaries

Learners use dictionaries to check meaning.

Example:

> ### 3 Vocabulary Development
>
> **Adjective–adverb link**
> **Can you find the adverbs which come from these adjectives? You can use your dictionary to help you.**
>
> | ADJECTIVE | ADVERB |
> |---|---|
> | obstinate | |
> | useful | |
> | fantastic | |
> | fast | |
> | good (better best) | |
> | bad (worse worst) | |
>
> **Sometimes it is easy to make an adverb from an adjective. Can you form any rules for doing this?**
> **You can form two adverbs from some adjectives in this list. Find them and write sentences to show you understand the different meanings.**
> **Some adjectives are exactly the same as their adverbs. Which ones?**
> **Can you think of any more to add to the list?**

Taken from *Mode 2*

Step 2   **P** and **C**

You need to choose your presentation technique according to the words you teach, since not every new word can be presented using each technique. For example, if the word is a small household object, like a *needle*, you can bring a needle into class; if the word is a concept, such as *cruelty*, you can't use realia to teach the word and so might use a situation or a story.

1 Work in pairs. Below are 12 words (a) to (l). Imagine you are going to present each one for the first time to an intermediate class of teenagers. Which of the techniques in *Step 1* would you use for each word? An example is provided below.

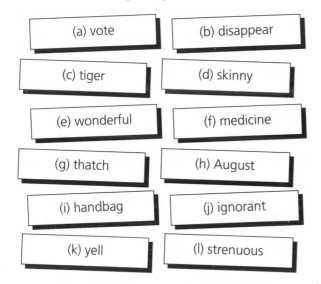

(a) vote	(b) disappear
(c) tiger	(d) skinny
(e) wonderful	(f) medicine
(g) thatch	(h) August
(i) handbag	(j) ignorant
(k) yell	(l) strenuous

Example:

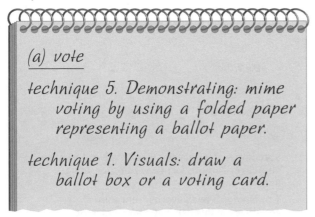

(a) vote

technique 5. Demonstrating: mime voting by using a folded paper representing a ballot paper.

technique 1. Visuals: draw a ballot box or a voting card.

2 As a whole class, role-play a few of your presentations to each other and discuss their effectiveness.

TASK 3 Double check   **G**

In this task, you practise concept checking. When you are teaching vocabulary, you need to ensure that your learners have understood the words you are teaching. You can do this by concept checking. This means that you ask simple questions using the new word(s), like this teacher is doing with the new word *bakery*:

Work in groups.

1 Imagine you have just presented the following new words:

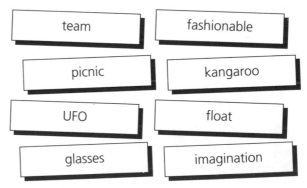

team	fashionable
picnic	kangaroo
UFO	float
glasses	imagination

2 In your group, divide up the words so each of you has *two* words to work on. It doesn't matter if the same word is used twice.

3 Individually, write down *four* concept checking questions for your own words that you could use to check understanding.

4 In your group, try out your concept checking questions on each other and comment on their effectiveness.

Lexical sets

TASK 4 Why lexical sets?   ▌

In this task, you read about lexical sets and the role they play in vocabulary teaching.

Work individually.

1 How do you think that we store words in our memory? Write some notes about this question.

2 Read the passage **Why lexical sets?** to discover one theory about how we store words.

WHY LEXICAL SETS?

What is a lexical set?

A lexical set (sometimes called a word set) is a cluster or group of related words.

How are words related in lexical sets?

Words can be related in several different ways, for example:

By topic	*furniture, clothes, family relationships, animals*
By similarity of meaning or synonymy	*gorilla, chimpanzee, orang-utang, ape*
In pairs – opposites	*hot/cold, old/new, hard/soft*
In pairs – synonyms	*slip/slide, rough/harsh, booklet/brochure*
In pairs – idioms	*black and white; black and blue*
In a series or a scale	*boiling, hot, warm, cool, cold, freezing*
By superordinates and hyponyms	superordinate: *FRUIT* hyponyms: *orange, apple, pineapple, banana, strawberry*
By activity or process	*steps in making a cake or building a bookcase*
Word families	*paint, painter, painting, paint work* OR *know, knowledge, knowing, knowledgeable, known*

Why are lexical sets important?

We probably don't store words in our brains in alphabetical order like a dictionary does. Research into memory has shown that we apparently store words in our brain in groups of related words (or lexical sets). Words that are related are somehow joined together in our brains; if a new word can be 'hooked' to words which are already stored, it might be easier to remember it. It would seem logical, therefore, that we should teach words in lexical sets to our learners, so that it is easier for them to retain and store the words in their memory. Task 5 deals with teaching a lexical set.

Microteaching

TASK 5 Choice of words[1]

This microteaching task practises writing a lesson plan for a lexical set and teaching it. If you are new to microteaching, read **3. Microteaching tasks** and **4. Feedback questions** on pages v-vi of the introduction.

Step 1   C

Work as a whole class.

Choose a lexical set of eight to ten related words for someone to teach to you.

Step 2   G and M

Work in groups.

1 Write a clear and detailed lesson plan to teach the lexical set you chose in Step 1 (your trainer will choose later on in the task who will teach: it might be you!). Use any vocabulary presentation and checking techniques that you like and as many techniques as you like. Look back at **Task 2 Mark my words** and **Task 3 Double check** for inspiration.

2 Make sure your plan is clear. The teacher must know exactly what to do at each stage of the lesson. Think about:

- when you want to hear, read, say and/or write the new words
- any helpful visuals
- concept-checking
- practice activities.

3 Experience the lesson. Your trainer will decide whose lesson plan to use for the microteaching and who will teach it; one trainee will teach the whole class.

Step 3   C

Work as a whole class.

Give feedback to the trainee who taught the words, using these Feedback questions as a guide.

Feedback questions

1 What in the lesson helped you?

2 What in the lesson hindered you?

3 Suggest improvements to the lesson so that the vocabulary learning might become more effective.

....

Further reading

Carter, Ronald and Michael McCarthy. (Eds.) 1988. *Vocabulary and Language Teaching*. Harlow: Addison Wesley Longman.
  An edited collection on aspects of vocabulary teaching.

Gairns, Ruth and Stuart Redman. 1986. *Working With Words*. Cambridge: Cambridge University Press.
  How to select, organise and teach vocabulary; includes both theory and practical activities.

Morgan, John and Mario Rinvolucri. 1986. *Vocabulary*. Oxford: Oxford University Press.
  Practical and original vocabulary learning activities.

Stevick, Earl W. 1976. *Memory, Meaning and Method*. Rowley, Massachusetts: Newbury House.
  A study of memory in language learning, including applications for language teaching.

[1] This is based on an idea from Woodward.

5 WARMING UP

Teaching the four skills: task preparation

Reading

TASK 1 Why warm up?

This reading introduces you to the reasons for using warming-up activities and their aims.

Step 1   P

Work in pairs. Discuss the following question before reading the text **Why warm up?**:

Why are warming-up activities important? Think of at least **three** reasons.

Step 2   I

Work individually.

Now read this text **Why warm up?** about warming-up activities and confirm or add to your original answers.

Why warm up?

This unit is about preparing our learners for language skills work. You will be introduced to various types of pre-skills (or warming-up) activities and, by the end of the unit, you will have experienced and evaluated several warming-up activities; you will also be able to design some pre-skills activities for your own learners. [1] [5]

The type of work your learners are going to do and the type of task you are teaching will, of course, influence which type of pre-skills activity you might choose. Some are short, others are long; some are content-based and others are language-based: your pre-skills activity will also depend on the amount of time you have and the importance you wish to place on each language skill. Of course, during the preparation stage, the learners will also be using English – perhaps talking about a picture or discussing a topic or learning new vocabulary. But by the time they do the language task, they should be well prepared for it. [10] [15] [20]

'Warming up' in real life

In real life, before you read, listen, watch, speak, or write, you already know a lot about what you are going to do. You have all kinds of expectations and predictions in your head. Even before you open a letter from a good friend who frequently corresponds with you, you usually have a reasonably clear idea about possible topics in that letter: you know who sent it, you know something about the events in their life and what kind of letters they usually write. When you write, you probably think about what you are going to write before you put pen to paper: if you are writing a report, you might plan each section carefully beforehand; if it is a quickly-scribbled note, you know who you are [25] [30] [35] writing to and what your message is. If you switch the radio on, you anticipate the kind of programme you are going to listen to: whether it will be news or drama or pop music; or you will tune the radio to your favourite station. When you meet someone, it is likely that you have anticipated some of the topics you might discuss and perhaps imagined some of the things you will say.

In the classroom, if a teacher turns on the tape recorder and says, *Listen to this*, without having introduced the topic of the tape, for example, it may be very difficult for the learners to understand what is happening on the tape. It can help our learners if we prepare them for language work, thus trying to replicate how they often read or listen or speak or write in real life.

In real life, in your own language, you are aware of many things before you communicate; other aspects of communication are unconscious. For example:

- you predict
- you expect
- you hope
- you know something about a topic
- you know the language you will use
- you are motivated to read
- you have a context or situation in which to communicate
- you are focused on what you are going to do
- you have a purpose for listening, reading, etc.
- you are personally involved.

We can relate this knowledge to teaching English by using warming-up activities with our learners, which helps them to contextualise their learning. This, in turn, may help them to be more successful learners.

Some aims of warming-up activities in class

The general goal of warming-up activities is to help learners learn better. Some more specific aims are:

- to create expectations about language, so that learners can understand better what is going to happen
- to give learners a reason to listen, read, speak or write
- to motivate learners to want to read or listen, speak or write
- to interest or intrigue learners in a topic
- to involve learners by asking for their ideas or knowledge about a topic
- to introduce or pre-teach vocabulary or difficult language which might otherwise prevent learners from understanding
- to introduce learners to the topic, for example by giving background information which is necessary for understanding or communicating
- to get learners communicating about the topic
- to draw attention to something of importance
- to focus learners (after a change in activity or if the lesson is beginning)
- to prepare learners with language to use during the activity
- to provide links between different stages of a lesson.

Pre-skills activities, therefore, aim to make language learning a more meaningful and effective experience so that learners can be successful in their learning in the classroom.

....

Observation

TASK 2 Do as I say

In this task, you discuss instruction giving and observe and reflect on a teacher's use of instructions.

Step 1   **G** and **C**

1 Work in groups. Make a list of factors which you consider to be important for effective instruction giving. For example:

clear voice quality, good eye contact, ...

2 As a class, collect together the factors you thought of in **1** and discuss how far they contribute to effective instruction giving.

3 Now look at the variables below. Are these the ideas you thought of? Add any more which you discussed and which you feel are important.

SOME VARIABLES IN INSTRUCTION GIVING

- clarity and simplicity of language
- voice quality
- body language and gesture
- use of visual aids
- checking understanding
- using L1 or L2
- your own teaching style

Step 2   I

Work individually.

Your trainer will give you a copy of the **Observation table: Instruction-giving skills** for each activity in the lesson. (Alternatively, if you have only one copy for all the activities, use a different-coloured pen each time.) Familiarise yourself with the table. Observe the instructions the teacher gives during the lesson and each time the teacher gives instructions for an activity, complete the table.

In the second column of the table are scales like this:

clear 4—3—2—1 *unclear*

For each skill you observe, *circle* the number on the scales to show how clear you feel the instruction giving skill is, as follows:

4 = very clear
3 = quite clear
2 = not very clear
1 = unclear

If you do *not* observe one of the skills, leave the scale blank.

In the right-hand column of the table, write in any comments which you feel are relevant to instruction giving.

Step 3   I

Work individually.

As soon as possible after your observation, answer the Post-observation questions in writing.

Post-observation questions

1 Summarise in one paragraph the instruction giving that you observed.

2 *a* In the activities you observed, was the instruction giving, in general, successful or unsuccessful?
b Add up your circled numbers to obtain an overall mark and comment on the mark.

3 In your opinion, which *three* elements from the left-hand column made the instruction giving particularly successful?

4 In your opinion, which *three* elements from the left-hand column made the instruction giving less successful?

5 Look at the scales in the centre column which you circled with a 2 or less. How might these aspects of instruction giving have been improved?

6 What are the most important factors for you personally in instruction giving?

7 What have you learnt for your own teaching after doing this observation task?

Step 4   C

Discuss your answers to the Post-observation questions in class or give them to your trainer.

Pre-reading

TASK 3 Before you read

In this task, you read about using magazine articles for teaching reading, as well as experiencing a pre-reading task for yourself.

Step 1   G

Work in groups.

1 You are going to read the first part of an article entitled **Reading tasks with magazines** from a magazine for English language teachers in secondary schools. What do you think the general topic of the article will be?

2 What do you think might be in the section entitled '**Using headlines**'?

3 What would you hope to learn in the section entitled '**Key words**'?

4 Below are some key words taken from the article. Based on these, what else do you think the article is about?

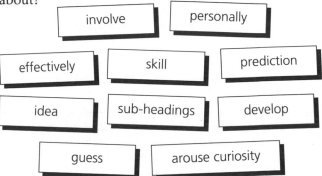

involve   personally   effectively   skill   prediction   idea   sub-headings   develop   guess   arouse curiosity

Reading tasks with magazines

In the third part of her series on using magazines in the language classroom Clare Lavery, who works with teachers in Italy and France, presents a variety of magazine activities designed to help your students read more effectively.

We rarely read a magazine article without having at least a vague idea of its content and interest for us – we use headlines, sub-headings, pictures and captions to think about the topic before reading. If students are given an article without preparation they may struggle through without focus. Here are some hints for preparing students before they read and to involve them personally in the reading process. All of the tasks are designed to arouse curiosity, to inject a puzzle element and to maintain students' interest.

Using headlines

Magazines use a variety of headlines and sub-headings for visual appeal and to give readers an idea of the layout of an article at a glance. They develop the skill of prediction, necessary for successful reading.

1   Take the sub-headings from an article (or invent your own) and put them in a jumbled list on the board. (See A). Ask students in pairs to use these to guess what the article is about. Ask questions such as *Why are these burgers green?* and *Where are hamburgers from?* You can also ask the class to give you suggestions for a main headline and then compare it to the original one in the magazine.

2   With a good class you can ask students in small groups to try and decide (looking at the sub-heading) what each paragraph will contain. The captions in magazines and newspapers are often a summary of the gist of the article and this trains learners to use them.

3   The sub-headings, if there are two or three, often break up the paragraphs in an article and give us an idea of its organisation. Ask students, in pairs or groups, to decide which paragraphs could be the introduction and which could be the conclusion. Using the example illustrated in class most students decided that 'Hamburger history' was the sub-heading for the first paragraph because it gives general background information about the birth of fast food. It is fun to do this if students can justify their choice.

Key words

If you make a list of the key words in an article they give us an idea of the story or general subject matter. In class they can give students support before reading and can be exploited to develop skills of prediction.

1   Here are some key words from two articles in different magazines:

> From an article about the British NHS:
> *treatment, Britain, resources, money, charges, doctors, nurses, patient, government, problems, efficiency*
>
> From an article about working as an au pair in the USA:
> *America, Europeans, money, work, visas, family, home exchanges, au pair, driving licence*

Students can be asked to guess what the article is about and then, if you wish, they can invent their own headline. After reading they may wish to change their headline in the light of what they have discovered.

2   You can take this activity a stage further by asking students in pairs to invent two sentences using the key words before they read. Collect suggestions from the whole class before reading the article. It is surprising how 'closely' the invented sentences match some of those encountered in the article.

3   If you leave the key words on the board, students can use them after reading as prompts for discussion or summary writing.

4   You can also ask students to read through an article and underline the key words. They should then compare their chosen words to their partner's. This focuses students' attention on getting the main ideas rather than concentrating too much on the detail or on unknown items.

Taken from *Practical English Teaching* Vol.12 no.2 December 1991

Step 2 **I**

Work individually.

Read the article **Reading tasks with magazines** (page 34). As you read, think about the predictions you made in Step 1: are they correct?

Step 3 **C** and **I** or **P**

Discuss these questions as a whole class.

1 How did the pre-reading activity in Step 1 help you to read the article more effectively?

2 *a* How has this task helped you to teach reading?
b How would you teach reading differently now?

3 Now work individually or in pairs.
a Find another text, either in this book or in a coursebook used in your teaching context.
b Create a pre-reading activity using key words or headlines for your chosen text.

4 Share your pre-reading activities with each other, either by posting them on the wall or copying them for each other.

....

Pre-listening

TASK 4 Forearmed

Below is a listening text from a book for beginners. On pages 36 and 37 are five different pre-listening activities, A to E, which you are going to evaluate in this task.

Taken from *Fountain Beginners Teacher's Book*

Step 1 **P**

Work in pairs.

1 Read the listening text, *Mrs Berry* below.

2 Read each pre-listening activity A–E (do not *do* every activity!), remembering that your learners will do pre-listening activities without seeing or hearing the listening text. The learners can see all the information that you have, except for the tapescript.

3 Complete the table on page 36, filling in the aim(s) of each activity and the skill(s) practised during each activity. One example has been done for you.

4 Which activity would you prefer, as learners? Give at least three reasons.

Listening text: Mrs Berry

Presenter: What did Mrs Berry have in her home in 1930? What didn't she have? Listen.

Girl: What was life like when you were a child, Grandma? Were things very different then?

Mrs Berry: Oh, yes. Very different. Life wasn't so easy in those days, you know. We didn't have a fridge. Only rich people had fridges then. We had to go shopping every day to buy fresh food. And we didn't have a washing machine. We washed all our clothes by hand in a big tub. It was very hard, very hard. We had electric light, though. Lots of people had electric light by then.

Girl: Did you have a television?

Mrs Berry: A television? Oh no! Ordinary people didn't have televisions in those days. But we had a radio – a great big radio. We all sat round the radio in the sitting-room, the whole family, listening to the news. And we had a record player, too. You had to wind it up, not like record players today. We listened to dance music.

Girl: What about a telephone? Did you have a telephone?

Mrs Berry: No, we didn't. Only rich people had telephones then, you know, not like today. We wrote letters in those days.

Girl: Did you have a car?

Mrs Berry: Yes, we had a car, a lovely little car. A lot of people had cars, even then – they weren't very expensive. We used to go for a drive every Sunday...

Pre-listening activity	Aim(s) of activity	Skill(s) practised
A Using pictures	1) *to contextualise the listening text* 2) *to motivate learners to want to listen*	*writing, speaking*
B Personalising		
C Predicting vocabulary		
D Predicting facts		
E Practising tenses		

Pre-listening activity A: Using pictures

Look at the photographs above. Work in pairs and write down your answers to the following questions:

1 How old are the people in the photographs, do you think?

2 In which years were they children?

3 Think about when they were children: how was life different for them, do you think?

4 What do you think they did in their spare time in the evenings? At the weekend?

5 How did they communicate?

Now listen to the tape and check if your answers are correct.

Pre-listening activity B: Personalising

The teacher talks about his own grandmother, who is 73, telling his class something about her childhood. He passes round photographs of his grandmother, as an old woman and as a child. He elicits from his class what they imagine about her childhood and particularly compares present-day electronic goods with what his grandmother might have had, or not had, as a child. He asks his learners to ask him questions about her and writes numbered statements that the learners make about his grandmother on the board (e.g. *1. She didn't have a television. 2. She had a washing machine.*). He then introduces the text by telling the class what Mrs Berry and her granddaughter are talking about: what life was like when Mrs Berry was her granddaughter's age. The teacher plays the listening text and the learners compare the statements on the board with the text to see if they are true or false or not mentioned.

Pre-listening activity C: Predicting vocabulary

The teacher says, *You are going to listen to a conversation between a girl and her grandmother, Mrs Berry. Her granddaughter is asking Mrs Berry what life was like in the 1930s, when Mrs Berry was a girl herself. Work in groups of four and together try to guess ten words which you think will hear in the conversation. For example, the words* radio *and* television. *Write the ten words in your notebooks.* Learners listen to the tape to check how many things they guessed.

Pre-listening activity D: Predicting facts

Discuss in pairs. Which of these things do you think ordinary British people had in their homes in 1930? Which ones didn't they have? Make two lists.

| fridge | washing machine | electric light | telephone |
| radio | television | record player | car |

THINGS PEOPLE HAD IN 1930   THINGS PEOPLE DIDN'T HAVE IN 1930

....

....

....

....

....

Now listen to the tape and check if your answers are correct.

Adapted from *Fountain* Learners' Book 1

Pre-listening activity E: Practising tenses

Look at the text below. Fill in the gaps. Choose the best answer from the box for each numbered gap. Some answers may be used more than once while others are not used at all.

| didn't | had | did | wasn't | was | have |

Girl: What was life like when you were a child, Grandma? Were things very different then?

Mrs Berry: Oh, yes. Very different. Life (1) _____ so easy in those days, you know. We (2) _____ have a fridge. Only rich people had fridges then. We had to go shopping every day to buy fresh food. And we (3) _____ have a washing machine. We washed all our clothes by hand in a big tub. It was very hard, very hard. We (4) _____ electric light, though. Lots of people (5) _____ electric light by then.

Girl: Did you (6) _____ a television?

Now listen to the tape and check if your answers are correct.

Step 2   **G**

Work in groups.

Reading and listening are both receptive skills, which means that the learners are receiving information (from texts) when they learn. Warming-up activities for the receptive skills can, therefore, be similar. Write down as many similarities as you can between warming-up activities for reading and listening.

Pre-writing and microteaching

TASK 5 Paving the way

The aims of this task are to examine some problems connected with writing, to think about solutions to those problems using pre-writing, and to design and teach a pre-writing activity.

Step 1   G

Work in groups.

1 Think about language classes where you have written something. Together, make a list of problems you encountered when you were learning to write in a foreign language.

Examples:

> *I couldn't think what to write.*
>
> *I wrote too informally.*

2 Some pre-writing activities can prevent learners from having some writing problems. Next to each problem, add a possible pre-writing activity which might help to solve it.

Examples:

Problem	Possible pre-writing activity
I couldn't think what to write.	*Brainstorm or gather together ideas in class.*
I wrote too informally.	*Give learners a model of what they are to write.*

Step 2   G

Work in groups.

Imagine your class is a group of 30 learners, aged 13-14, who have been learning English for one or two years. Here is your learners' writing task:

> **Writing Task: Coming Home**
>
> Jerry, a 14-year-old, arrives home. His parents told him to be home by 7 o'clock and it is now 11 o'clock. Write the dialogue between Jerry and his parents, just after he comes in the door.

1 Your trainer will give you a pre-writing activity, A, B, C or D.

2 Design your group's pre-writing activity. Your activity should help your learners in some way to write their dialogue.

3 Use the Focus questions to help you think about your pre-writing activity.

Focus questions

1 What activity will the learners do?

2 How exactly will you set up your activity?

3 Will the learners work individually, in pairs, in small groups or as a whole class?

4 Which language skill(s) will they practise?

5 How long will your activity be?

6 What are the precise aims of your activity?

Step 3   M and C

If you are new to microteaching, read **3. Microteaching tasks** and **4. Feedback questions** on pages v-vi of the introduction.

Work as a whole class.

Each group chooses one representative to teach the activity: the rest of the group observes but does not participate. Teach the pre-writing activity as if the class are teenagers: pay particular attention to instruction giving. Each group in turn has a maximum of ten minutes to microteach their pre-writing activity or part of their activity.

After each group has done some microteaching, discuss the following Feedback questions in groups.

Feedback questions

1 How well did each pre-writing activity help you, as learners, to prepare for the writing activity?

2 Was the pre-writing activity enjoyable and motivating? Why/why not?

3 Comment on the instructions given for the activity.

4 What would you add to the activity if it were taught again?

5 What would you leave out of the activity?

6 Suggest one practical improvement for the teaching of the pre-writing activity.

Pre-speaking

TASK 6 Before you open your mouth...

In this task, you evaluate pre-speaking activities.

Step 1   P

Work in pairs.

1 Look at this speaking activity:

2 Roleplay

Part 1
Student A   Study role 1
Student B   Study role 2
Act out the situation.

Role 1

It's Saturday afternoon and you are doing nothing. You phone a new friend who you met quite recently and greet him/her. Ask your friend what she/he is doing. Explain that you phoned last night and that the friend wasn't at home. Ask where she/he was. Explain that there's a party on a certain date. Invent the day, date and time of the party. Invite your friend to the party. Accept an invitation to go to his/her house this afternoon. Finish the conversation.

Role 2

It's Saturday afternoon and you are doing your homework when your new friend phones you. Answer the phone. (Invent a phone number). Last night you went to the cinema. (What film did you see? Who did you go with? Was the film good?). You are not sure if you want to go to the party with your friend. You want to find out more about the party. Ask your friend what she/he is doing and invite him/her to your house this afternoon. Finish the conversation.

Taken from
Mode 1

2 On pages 40-41, there are four different pre-speaking activities, A–D, which your learners might do before they do the role-play. Read quickly through these.

3 Complete the columns **Skill(s) practised**, **Grouping** and **Aim(s)** in the table on page 40, referring to the four pre-speaking activities, A–D. (Ignore the **Rank** column for the moment.) For each speaking activity, write in:

- the skill(s) that each pre-speaking activity practises
- the groupings required (whole class, pairs, groups)
- the aim(s) of each activity.

Some examples are given for you in the table.

Pre-speaking activity	Skill(s) practised	Grouping	Aim(s)	Rank
A Eliciting ideas			*raising interest in the topic; reminding learners what language they can use*	
B Listening to a dialogue	*listening, speaking*			
C Using key words		*pairs*		
D Using photographs				

Pre-speaking activity A: Eliciting ideas

The teacher asks about a situation which is similar to the role-play in the book. She uses questions to elicit from the learners similar information to the situation, for example: *You have just met a new friend and want to go somewhere with him or her. You telephone him/her to invite him/her out. Where are you going? What else are you going to talk about? How do you feel about the situation?* The teacher then explains the role-play and gives out the role cards. Learners choose which role they would like to play; before they begin, each learner writes some questions that they will ask each other in their notebooks.

Pre-speaking activity B: Listening to a dialogue

The teacher records a telephone conversation on to a cassette, asking two colleagues to role-play the two characters in the book's role-play. She hands out the questions below to the learners, who listen to the dialogue and answer the questions individually; they then compare their answers in pairs.

THE PHONE CONVERSATION

1 Why does the man phone the woman?
2 How does the woman feel about being telephoned?
3 What did the woman do last night?
4 What are they going to do together?

The learners read their role cards and the role-play begins.

Pre-speaking activity C: Using key words

The teacher writes some key words from the role-play on the board, for example:

phone   at home   party   film   invitation   homework   cinema

She asks the learners to write a dialogue in pairs, containing all the words on the board. Some learners read their dialogues aloud to the whole class. Finally, the teacher gives the role cards out.

Pre-speaking activity D: Using photographs

The teacher finds two photos of individuals on the phone and shows them to her class. She reminds her learners how British people answer the phone (stating the number) and how they greet each other. She introduces the situation: *You have just met each other. One of you is phoning the other to invite them to go to a party.*
You will work in pairs, with role cards. Here are the role cards...

Step 2 [I] and [P]

1 Work individually.

Decide which pre-speaking activity you would like best *to teach*, which you would like second best, and so on. In the **Rank** column of the table on page 40, number the activity you like most 1, the second one 2, etc.

2 Work in pairs.

a Discuss your answers to question 1, giving reasons for your first and last choices.
b How do you feel the pre-speaking activity that you ranked number 1 would prepare your learners to prepare to speak effectively?

c Is there a difference between the one you prefer and the one you feel would be most effective? Explain why.

Step 3

Work in groups.

Speaking and writing are both productive skills: learners have to actively produce something when they speak and write. Warming-up activities for the productive skills can, therefore, be similar. Write down as many similarities as you can between warming-up activities for speaking and writing.

Further reading

Grellet, Francoise. 1981. *Developing Reading Skills.* Cambridge: Cambridge University Press. 'Sensitising' pp 28-53.
   Includes some warming-up activities to use with reading texts.

Grundy, Peter. 1993. *Newspapers.* Oxford: Oxford University Press.
   Many pre-skills activities to use with newspaper articles.

Hess, Nathalie. 1991. *Headstarts: One Hundred Original Pre-Text Activities.* Harlow: Pilgrims-Addison Wesley Longman.
   A hundred ideas for pre-reading activities.

Nuttall, Christine. 1996 (New edition). *Teaching Reading Skills in a Foreign Language.* Oxford: Heinemann. Chapter 2: 'Reading for what purpose?'
   Discusses reasons for reading.

Ur, Penny. 1984. *Teaching Listening Comprehension.* Cambridge: Cambridge University Press. Chapter 1: 'Real-life listening.'
   Lists what we listen to in real life and how listening in real life is related to classroom teaching.

6 NOW HEAR THIS!
Teaching listening

Reflection

TASK 1 All ears

In this task, you compare listening to English inside the classroom and listening to your first language in real life.

Step 1

Work in groups.

Complete the Listening Mind Map on page 43; it compares listening to L1 *outside* the classroom with listening to English *inside* the classroom. Use the prompts written on the branches to help you and add other branches if you like. A few examples have been done for you.

Step 2

Work in groups.

Discuss your answers to the Focus questions.

Focus questions

1 What are the differences between listening to L1 outside the classroom and listening to English inside the classroom? Give at least *three* examples.

2 How can a teacher make the purpose of a listening activity clear to the learners?

3 How can a teacher create a context for a listening passage? Give at least *three* examples.

4 How can a teacher help to reduce learners' worries or negative feelings about listening in the classroom? Suggest at least *three* ways.

Step 3

Discuss your answers to Step 2 as a class.

Listening Mind Map

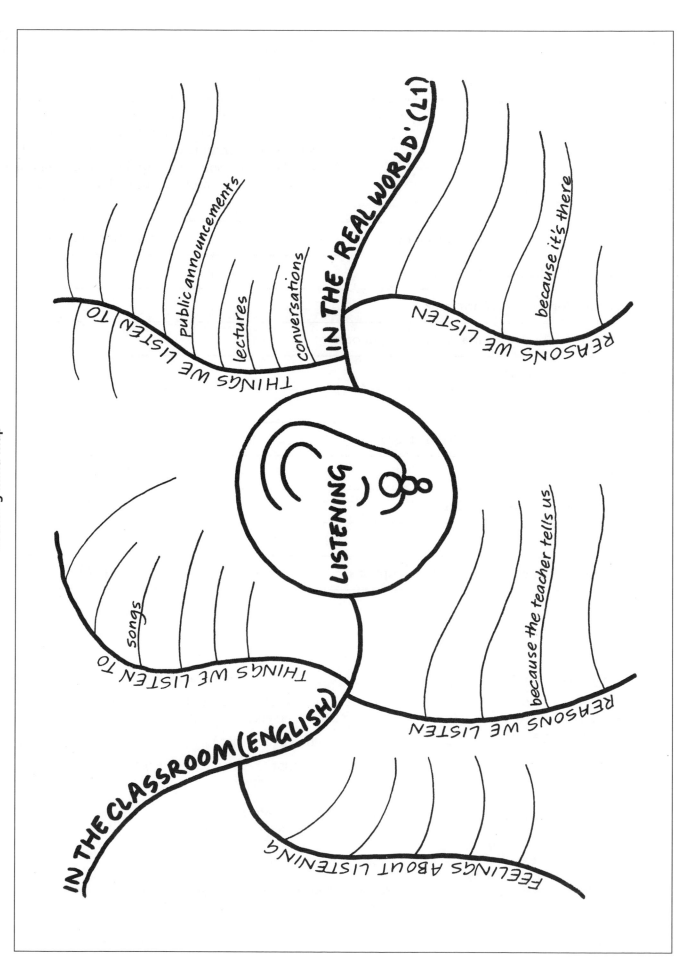

IN THE 'REAL WORLD' (L1)

THINGS WE LISTEN TO
- public announcements
- lectures
- conversations

REASONS WE LISTEN
- because it's there

LISTENING

REASONS WE LISTEN
- because the teacher tells us

IN THE CLASSROOM (ENGLISH)

THINGS WE LISTEN TO
- songs

FEELINGS ABOUT LISTENING

Listening tasks

TASK 2　Using an ear trumpet

In this task you examine and evaluate ten listening activities and decide on their aims.

Step 1　**P**

Work in pairs.

Match each of the Listening aims (1-10) in the table below with the instructions to the learner in Listening activities A-J (pp. 44-46), by writing the letter of one or more activities (A-J) in the right-hand column. Some aims apply to more than one activity. One example has been done for you.

Listening aims	Listening activity
1　Listening for the main ideas / gist	
2　Listening for specific information	
3　Listening to check if your answers are right or not	
4　Listening to check for mistakes	
5　Listening for dictation	
6　Listening to re-order a jumbled dialogue	
7　Listening to take notes	
8　Listening to complete a picture	
9　Listening to other learners	
10　Listening to match pictures with descriptions	*H, D*

Listening activity A

Listen to the story about Michael's big surprise. Write down what Michael's big surprise is.

Listening activity B

Listen to the sequence of sounds on the cassette. Make a list of the things you heard, e.g. *a baby crying*, *a door closing*. In pairs, compare lists.

Adapted from *Mode 3*

Listening activity C

Listen to two conversations. What's the time in each conversation? Write the times in numbers.

(Learners cannot see tapescript.)

Presenter:　Tapescript 42. Listen and write the times. Conversation 1.
Burglar 1:　What's the time?
Burglar 2:　Ssh!
Burglar 1:　What's the time?
Burglar 2:　It's twenty-five to four.

Presenter:　Conversation 2.
Man:　Excuse me. Could you tell me the time, please?
Woman:　Yes, of course. It's quarter to three.
Man:　Thank you.

Adapted from *Fountain Beginners Teacher's Book*

Listening activity D

On the phone

Look at the picture and listen to ten sentences.
Say together, 'Yes, that's right' or 'No, that's wrong'

Example: The café is number 3.
You say: No, that's wrong.

Adapted from *Mosaic 1*

Listening activity E

Answer these questions about Susan's room. As you listen, note down either *Yes, she has* or *No, she hasn't*.

1 Has Susan got a big bookcase? *Yes, she has.*

2 Has she got a picture of a kangaroo on the wall? *No, she hasn't.*

3 Has she got an easel?

4 Has she got two pianos?

5 Has she got a cassette player?

Adapted from *Fountain Beginners*

Listening activity G

Show your project to your teacher and your friends. Look at your friends' projects and talk about them.

Taken from *Mosaic 1*

Listening activity F

1. Here is a dialogue between Anna and Mr Baker. Read it to yourself and put it in the right order.

Mr Baker: Five pencils, two exercise books, a rubber, and... how many envelopes?

Anna: Can I have a newspaper, please?

Mr Baker: Hello, Anna. I'm fine thanks. And you?

Anna: Hello, Mr Baker. How are you?

Mr Baker: Yes, certainly. Here you are.

Anna: Thank you. And can I have ... let's see ... five pencils, two exercise books, a rubber and, er, ten envelopes.

Mr Baker: Good.

Anna: Ten, please.

Anna: I'm OK, thanks.

Mr Baker: Right. Here you are. Anything else?

2. Now listen to the dialogue. Did you have the right order?

Adapted from *Mosaic 1*

Listening activity H

Listen to the tape and put the dialogue in the right order.
Then match a–g with Dave's family.

Example:

a This is my brother Peter.
Is he nice?
No, he isn't. He's horrible.

a
| This is my brother Peter. |
| Is he nice? |
| No, he isn't. He's horrible. |

b
| Who's this? |
| My grandfather. |

c
| This is my sister Jane. |
| Is she nice? |
| Yes, she is. |

d
| This is my father. He isn't tall and thin. |
| No, he's short and fat. |

e
| And this is me. I'm young and I'm nice. |
| Oh, yes? |

f
| Is this your mother? |
| Yes, it is. |
| She's tall and thin. |
| Yes, she is. |

g
| And this is my grandmother. |
| She's old. |
| Yes, she is. But she's nice. |

1st	c
2nd	
3rd	
4th	
5th	
6th	
7th	

1   2   3   4   5   6   7

Taken from *Mosaic 1*

Listening activity I

Listen and write the missing words.

A Where's Peter _____?

B _____'s from G_____.

A Is Mary from _____?

B No. _____ isn't.
   S_____ from _____ _____.

Adapted from *Mosaic 1*

Listening activity J

Copy the plan of the empty living room. In the conversation you will hear, a man and a woman are moving house and are bringing their furniture into their living room; as they talk, draw in the furniture. Draw the two sofas, the lamps, the coffee table, the mat, the bookcase, the stereo and the television.

Step 2   **G**

Work in groups.

Discuss the Focus questions.

Focus questions

1 Look at the Listening activities A–J again.

   a Which of the activities require a silent response (e.g., drawing, writing)?
   b Which activities require the learners to answer with a short (spoken or written) response?
   c Which require a longer answer?
   d What are some advantages of making short responses during or immediately after listening?
   e What are some disadvantages of making long responses during or immediately after listening?

2 **a** Which Listening activity A–J do you prefer?
   b Why?

3 **a** Think of, or find, three *other* types of listening activities (e.g. from coursebooks).
   b What is the aim of each type of task?
   c Give *one* advantage and *one* disadvantage of each of the listening activities you found?

Observation

TASK 3 Eavesdropping on a teacher

In this task you observe a listening lesson, in order to think about the learners' success in listening and to reflect upon possible ways of improving that success.

Step 1

Work individually.

1 Your trainer will give you a copy of the **Observation table: Teaching listening**. You will also need a watch.

2 Arrange to observe a class where the learners will listen.

3 Complete the **Observation table: Teaching listening**, noting in the appropriate columns:

- the kind of preparation the learners do for listening
- the time spent on preparing learners to listen
- the learners' purpose in listening: was it stated by the teacher?
- the type, topic and length of listening passage
- the number of times learners listened to the same text or part of the text.

4 As soon as possible after your observation, write your answers to the Post-observation questions in Step 2.

Step 2

Work individually.

Answer the Post-observation questions in writing.

Post-observation questions

1 *a* What preparation (i.e. pre-listening activity) were the learners given before they listened to the passage? If they had some preparation, answer (b); if they did not, answer (c).
b How did the pre-listening activity help them to understand better?
c What pre-listening activity might have been done to help them understand the text better?

2 *a* Did the learners experience a while-listening activity, or more than one? If so, answer (b); if not, answer (c).
b What were the aims of the while-listening activity/activities?
c What while-listening activity might have helped the learners to listen?

3 *a* Did the learners experience a post-listening activity, or more than one? If so, answer (b); if not, answer (c).
b What were the aims of the post-listening activity/activities?
c What post-listening activity (or activities) might have helped the learners to understand what they had heard?

4 *a* How many times did the learners listen?
b How much more would the learners have understood if they had been allowed to listen to the text again? Explain.
c Did the learners hear the whole text at once? If so, was that helpful? If not, would that be more helpful?

5 *a* What are the three advantages for teachers and learners of using the model of pre-, while- and post-listening activities to teach a listening lesson?
b What are two disadvantages for teachers and learners of using this model (pre-, while- and post-listening activities) to teach a listening lesson?

Listening

TASK 4 And the winner is... **P**

In this activity you evaluate techniques for teaching listening.

Work in pairs.

1 Your trainer will give you a copy of the table **Teaching listening techniques**.

Score the teaching listening techniques in the table according to your own opinion. Use this scale:

> 1 = very effective
> 2 = rather effective
> 3 = rather ineffective
> 4 = completely ineffective

2 In the table, write the advantages and disadvantages of each technique. The first example has been done for you.

3 Be prepared to tell the rest of the class which techniques you thought the most effective and which the least effective, and why.

Microteaching

TASK 5 Tune in

In this task you prepare and teach or experience a pre-listening, while-listening or post-listening activity. If you are new to microteaching, read **3. Microteaching tasks** and **4. Feedback questions** on pages v–vi of the introduction.

Step 1 **G** and **P**

Work in a group of 6.

1 Find a listening text you would like to use in a listening lesson; you will need a copy of the tape and the tapescript.

2 Divide into three pairs and prepare the following:

Pair A: a pre-listening activity
Pair B: a while-listening activity
Pair C: a post-listening activity

Each activity should last no more than five minutes.

Work with your partner to prepare to teach your activity, including any extra materials necessary. Decide who is teaching what.

3 Together, read through all of your activities and suggest improvements to them before you teach.

Step 2 **M**

1 Teach your activities to your class.

2 Tell them, at the beginning, the level and age of learners for whom you designed the lesson and the aims of your activity. Keep to your five-minute time limit for each part of the lesson.

3 Have a feedback session, focusing on teaching listening; discuss both the strengths and possible improvements to your activities.

Time out, take five

Journal entry
If I had only known then what I know now...

How have your ideas about teaching listening and learning to listen changed since you began the unit? How would you approach a listening lesson differently now?

What remaining questions or concerns do you have about teaching listening?

Further reading

Beckerman, H. 1989. *Guessworks! A Musical Mystery Play*. New York: Collier Macmillan.
  A theatrical approach to listening, incorporating text, music, and lyrics (intermediate level).

Cornelius, E.T., Jr. 1981. *Interview*. New York: Addison Wesley Longman.
  Bases listening tasks on ten authentic interviews with Americans workers (high-intermediate-advanced).

Morgan, J. and M. Rinvolucri. 1983. *Once Upon a Time*. Cambridge: Cambridge University Press.
  Suggests many creative ways to use story-telling in class.

Murphey, Tim. 1992. *Music and Song.* Oxford: Oxford University Press.
  Lots of ideas for using music and song in listening and other lessons.

Rinvolucri, M. and P. Davis. 1988. *Dictation: New Methods, New Possibilities*. Cambridge: Cambridge University Press.
  A fresh look at dictation, with many creative activities suggested.

Rost, M. 1990. *Listening in Language Learning*. Harlow: Addison Wesley Longman.
  Covers background issues in listening, with numerous examples and questions.

Ur, P. 1984. *Teaching Listening Comprehension*. Cambridge: Cambridge University Press.
  Contains an elaborate taxonomy of listening task types and thorough analysis of the listening process.

Swartz, B.F. and R. L. Smith. 1986. *This is a Recording: Listening with a Purpose*. Englewood Cliffs, N.J.: Prentice-Hall, Inc.
  Presents numerous tasks based on recorded telephone messages (intermediate-level).

7 SPEAKING YOUR MIND
Teaching speaking

Reflection

TASK 1 Talking of speaking

In this task you practise speaking and become more aware of some of the issues in teaching speaking.

Step 1

Work as a whole class.

1 Read the **Find someone who...** statements about speaking activities in the box on the opposite page.

2 Walk around the classroom and find at least one person in your class who agrees with each statement. Write their name next to the statement that they agree with.

3 There is one rule: you can only ask *two* questions to one person at a time. You must then change partners and ask someone else another question.

Step 2 G

Work in groups.

What do you think makes a good speaking class? Write down at least two criteria for a good speaking class under each of the following five headings: **the teacher, the learners, the atmosphere, correction, activities**. Then give reasons for each criterion, e.g.

The learners
- *need to be tolerant of each other.*
Why?
- *they might be shy or embarrassed if they are scared of other learners.*

Step 3

Have a class discussion and add to your own list of criteria and reasons, by sharing your ideas so far with each other about speaking classes.

STATEMENT	NAME
Find someone who...	
... likes pair work.	
... enjoys drills.	
... doesn't like creating a dialogue and acting it out.	
... doesn't like speaking in front of the whole class.	
... likes it when one student reads aloud to the whole class from a text.	
... likes speaking classes where one learner gives a talk.	
... enjoys speaking foreign languages with his or her classmates, even out of class.	
... dislikes role-plays.	
... likes discussion classes where the whole class discusses a topic together.	
... likes activities using visuals.	
... enjoys group work.	
... likes guessing games.	
... enjoys using questionnaires.	
... likes drama activities.	

Speaking activities

TASK 2 Filling the gap

In this task, you learn about information-gap activities.

Step 1   C

Work as a whole class.

Discuss the following:

1 What do you think are the characteristics of an information-gap activity?

2 Why are information-gap activities important in teaching speaking?

Step 2   P

Work in pairs.

Discuss these questions:

1 *a* Was the activity **Find someone who...** in **Task 1** an information-gap activity?
   b Why/why not?

2 *a* On page 52 are four speaking activities (A–D). Which of them are information-gap activities?
   b Why/why not?

Speaking activity A: Completing a questionnaire

Learners have created the questionnaire below about their teacher. They ask the teacher the questions and complete their questionnaires.

Question	Answer
1 Are you married?	*Yes*
2 Do you have children?	
3 If so, how many?	
4 What are their names?	
5 Where do you live?	

Speaking activity B: Having a discussion

Learners work in groups of four. They have a discussion, answering the questions below. They then tell the rest of the class what they decided.

What would you do if...

1. ... someone fainted in class?

2. ... you left your English homework at home?

3. ... you forgot that your Mum wanted you to babysit and you had arranged to go to the cinema with a friend?

4. ... someone offered you a free year at an English school?

Adapted from *Fountain Elementary*

Speaking activity C: Reading a dialogue aloud

Read the dialogue from your book aloud in pairs, learner A playing Mandy and learner B playing Detective Sergeant Bright.

Taken from *Mode 1*

Speaking activity D: Creating and reading a weather forecast

By yourself, write a weather forecast for the UK tomorrow. Then read your weather forecast to your partner. Can he/she draw the weather map of the UK correctly?

TASK 3 Talking the hind leg off a donkey

In this task, you evaluate three speaking activities.

Step 1 **P**

Work in pairs. Your trainer will give you a copy of the table **Talking the hind leg off a donkey**.

Look at the three speaking activities (A–C). Imagine you are going to teach them. Look at each one and complete the table by writing a brief comment about each activity in the appropriate square. Some examples are done for you.

Step 2 **P**

Work in pairs and do *one* of the following tasks:

1 Write a short lesson plan for teaching one of the three speaking activities. (For help with lesson planning, look at **Unit 13 Plan of attack**.)

2 Design a pre-speaking activity to prepare your class for one of the activities (A–C).

Speaking activity A

B Give instructions to your partner on how to draw this picture. Start like this: Draw a rectangle. Make the top and bottom 12 cm long and the sides 9 cm…

Taken from *Say the Word*

Speaking activity B

3 Roleplay

In pairs.
Student A You are the mother or father.
Student B You are Student A's son or daughter. Look at page 127.
Read your roles and act out the situation.

Student A

You are Student B's mother or father. You are going away to Barry Island for the weekend. You are leaving on Friday evening at seven o'clock and coming back on Sunday night for dinner at eight o'clock. The telephone number of the Barry Island Excelsior Hotel is 572 9743. While you are away you want your son or daughter to do some things for you. These are the things: Friday evening: do the shopping and feed the cat. Saturday morning: cut the grass in the garden – afternoon: do the cleaning, – evening: visit your grandmother. Sunday morning: tidy your room – afternoon: wash the car – evening: prepare dinner.

Student B

You are Student A's son or daughter. Your parents are going away for the weekend. Ask them when they are leaving and when they are coming back. Also ask them for the phone number of the hotel they are staying at. You have got a busy weekend. You don't like doing housework. You have got a lot of homework this weekend. On Friday night you're going dancing. On Saturday afternoon you're playing volleyball with friends. On Saturday evening you're going to the cinema. On Sunday morning and evening you are going to do your homework and on Sunday afternoon you're going to invite some friends to your house to listen to music.

Taken from *Mode 1*

Speaking activity C

5 Parent power

Answer the questions in the column YOU. Ask another student the questions and put his or her answers in the column YOUR PARTNER.

	YOU	YOUR PARTNER
Do your parents let you		
stay out late?		
go to discos?		
invite friends home?		
drink alcohol?		
smoke?		
choose your own clothes?		
Do they make you		
keep your room tidy?		
stay at home and study?		
go out with them at weekends?		
lay the table?		
go shopping with them?		
Do they want you		
to get high marks at school?		
to go to university?		
to leave school and get a job?		
to get a job in the holidays?		
to do the same things as your brother/sister?		
to become independent?		

Taken from *Mode 2*

TASK 4 Talking shop

This task aims to get you thinking about how to teach a specific speaking activity.

Step 1   **P**

Work in pairs.

Opposite is a speaking activity, *'When's your birthday?'*

This is how one teacher prepared her class to do this activity. Read what she says and discuss the following questions:

1 What do you like about her preparation?

2 What would you change in her preparation?

I first asked my class, *What's the date today?* One learner replied, *The third of September.* I explained that she was right and wrote the full form of the date on the board: the third of September. I pointed out the difference between how the date is written (September 3rd) and how we say it in English, *the third of September.* I wrote down some dates on the board: February 28th, October 1st, April 15th and the class repeated them in chorus. They wrote down four more dates in their books and gave these to their partners and their partners said them. Then they listened to a short conversation on a tape among six school friends talking about birthdays and had to write the birthdays beside the names.

Finally each learner wrote down the names of five people in the class who weren't sitting near to them; everyone stood up and had to ask those five people what their birthdays were, doing the exercise *When's your birthday?* from their textbook. While they asked and answered questions, I moved around the class, listening to what they were saying and encouraging them to speak English when they slipped into L1. It was a bit noisy, but they worked hard. Before they left, I asked some of them to tell the rest of the class the dates of some of their classmates' birthdays. For homework, they wrote down in English the birthdays of five of the people in their families.

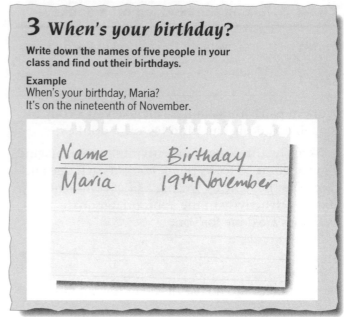

3 When's your birthday?

Write down the names of five people in your class and find out their birthdays.

Example
When's your birthday, Maria?
It's on the nineteenth of November.

Name	Birthday
Maria	19th November

Taken from *Mode 1*

Step 2   **P**

Work in pairs.

Look at Speaking activity C **Parent power** in **Task 3 Talking the hind leg off a donkey** (p. 53). Imagine you are going to teach the activity. Your class is a class of 30 thirteen-year-olds, who mostly enjoy speaking activities; they are lively, and usually cooperate.

Discuss the Focus questions to help you to decide how to teach **Parent power**.

Focus questions

1 What grammar and/or vocabulary will your learners need to know before doing this activity?

2 What will you do to prepare and motivate your class for the pair work?

3 How exactly will you divide your class up and at what stage?

4 What examples will you give to your learners?

5 What instructions will you give your class to help them understand what to do? State exactly what you will say.

6 What will you do during the activity (e.g. correct them, listen in, sit at the front)?

7 What will you do when everyone has finished?

8 What will you do as a follow-on from the activity to help the learners consolidate what they have been learning?

Microteaching

TASK 5 Chatterbox

In this task, you teach or are taught a speaking activity. If you are new to microteaching, read **3. Microteaching tasks** and **4. Feedback questions** on pages v–vi of the introduction.

Step 1

One of you is the teacher, and the others are the learners. Read your instructions: your trainer will provide the teacher's instructions, and the learners' instructions are below.

Learners' instructions

One of your classmates is going to teach you a speaking activity. While she is teaching, make notes on the following aspects of her teaching and be prepared to give some feedback to her on:

a   how she gives instructions

b   how much English the teacher and learners speak during the activity

c   what she does during the pair work

d   how she starts and stops the activity

e   what she does after the activity.

Step 2 G

Work in groups.

Discuss the feedback to be given to the teacher, using the Feedback questions. The aim of feedback is to help someone improve, so be tactful.

Feedback questions

1   Discuss the points about the microteaching that you observed during the activity in the **Learners' instruction** box.

2   Choose two more things to say to your classmate who taught the activity as feedback:

a one thing about her teaching that you liked
b one improvement that could be made in her teaching.

Step 3

Give feedback to your classmate about her teaching.

TASK 6 They've lost their tongues

In this task you discuss problems of teaching speaking and think about possible solutions.

Step 1 C

A common problem in speaking classes is that some learners don't say much in their classes, even if they are asked to. Why don't they? What problems have you met in speaking classes, either as a teacher or a learner? As a class, list some typical problems to do with teaching speaking, e.g. *Some learners refuse to speak English.*

Step 2

Work in pairs.

Read the teachers' statements (1–7) and the possible solutions for these problems (a–k) on page 56. Match each problem to one or more solutions: more than one solution might be possible.

Statements

1   *My class says they don't have anything to say and don't like speaking English.*

2   *My learners say they can't talk because they'll make lots of mistakes.*

3   *My learners say their friends will laugh at them if they talk.*

4   *My learners say they don't know how to say anything in English.*

5   *My pupils just don't understand what they should do in group work; I've given up!*

6   *My pupils are all really shy and daren't say anything. They say they aren't good enough.*

7   *My class just speaks in their own language if we do group work.*

Possible solutions

a Keep speaking as much English as you, yourself, can, so your class gets used to hearing English in the classroom.

b Teach learners the necessary language for the activity, or revise it; practise an example with them first.

c Ask a learner to repeat the instructions of an activity to the rest of the class.

d Don't correct all mistakes: in some speaking classes, encourage learners to speak but don't correct their English continually while they are speaking.

e Correct mistakes at the end of an activity (you can collect a list as you go around the class listening).

f Teach your class 'helping' language e.g., 'How do you say .... in English?' 'It's my turn.'

g Repeat instructions in a different way in case some learners weren't listening or didn't quite understand.

h Encourage your learners to support each other; discourage learners who laugh at others.

i Give your learners a lot of encouragement and praise. For example, say 'Well done!' or 'You did really well during that activity.'

j Tell your learners very specifically WHY it is important to speak English in class or discuss with them why they don't want to speak English.

k Ask some learners to do an example together in front of the class.

Step 3

Work in groups.

Read the case study below and then answer the Focus questions.

Focus questions

1 Describe the problem with Emil.

2 Why do you think this problem exists?

3 Think of at least **three** different solutions for the problem.

CASE STUDY

I teach a class of fourteen-year-olds and recently I have been introducing more speaking into our classes. Pair work activities usually work quite well, but a few weeks ago I started to try group work, where the learners work together in groups of three or four. Again, most learners seem to like it and try to talk English. But there are some problematic students in the group. My main problem is Emil: if we do group work, he dominates the group and talks a lot and loudly in (L1) but doesn't say much in English unless I go to his group and stand there listening. He says he's not very interested, but I know he could perform much better. Maybe I should just give up this group work – it just doesn't work.

Game

TASK 7 The atmosphere game

The aim of this game is to practise creating a comfortable atmosphere in your classes.

Step 1 **C**

Work as a whole class.

Brainstorm ways in which English teachers you have known have established a good atmosphere where learners have felt able to contribute, particularly in speaking lessons.

Step 2

Work in groups.

Play '**The atmosphere game**'.

Materials per group (provided by your trainer):

- one copy of the board
- two dice
- one copy of rules of 'The atmosphere game'
- 1 counter per player

Step 3   G

Work in the same group. Write down ten pieces of advice for teachers on establishing a good atmosphere for successful speaking activities.

Example:

> *Explain to your learners why you want them to speak English to each other.*

Time out, take five

> *Journal entry*
> ### Writing about speaking
>
> Thinking about the problems you discussed in the unit about teaching speaking, write about whether you have found solutions to these problems.
>
> What more would you like to learn about teaching speaking, now that you have completed this unit?

Further reading

Doughty, Catherine and Teresa Pica. 1986. '"Information gap" tasks: do they facilitate second language acquisition?' *TESOL Quarterly, 20:2*.
   Article about research done into how information gap tasks might affect language acquisition.

Hopson, Barrie and Mike Scally. 1981. *Lifeskills Teaching*. London: McGraw-Hill.
   Interesting sections on working with groups in the classroom and how to establish a positive climate.

Klippel, Friederike. 1984. *Keep Talking*. Cambridge: Cambridge University Press.
   Lots of ideas for speaking activities at all levels.

Krashen, Stephen D and Tracy D Terrell. 1983. *The Natural Approach*. Oxford: Pergamon/Alemany.
   Krashen and Terrell's ideas on teaching speaking, including Krashen's affective filter theory.

Long, Michael and Patricia Porter. 1985. 'Group work, interlanguage talk, and second language acquisition.' *TESOL Quarterly, 19:2*.
   Important article on research done into group work and how it might affect language acquisition.

Moskowitz, Gertrude. 1976. *Caring and Sharing in the Foreign Language Class*. Cambridge, Mass: Newbury House.
   Lots of ideas for humanistic speaking activities.

Nolasco, Rob and Lois Arthur. 1987. *Conversation*. Oxford: Oxford University Press.
   Ideas for speaking activities at all levels.

Porter-Ladousse, Gillian. 1987. *Role Play*. Oxford: Oxford University Press.
   Many ideas for using role-plays.

Puchta, Herbert and Michael Schratz. 1993. *Teaching Teenagers*. Harlow: Pilgrims-Addison Wesley Longman.
   Communicative activities which have really worked with teenagers.

Willis, Jane. 1981. *Teaching English Through English*. Harlow: Addison Wesley Longman.
   A book which very explicitly helps teachers with using English in their lessons.

8 BETWEEN THE LINES

Teaching reading

Observation

TASK 1 Private eye

In this observation task you investigate what, how and why people read in real life (i.e., outside the classroom) and contrast this with reading English in the classroom.

Step 1 ∎

Work individually.

Your trainer will give you a copy of the **Observation table: Real-life reading**. Complete the task within a 48-hour period, observing at least ten people who are reading something (not necessarily English nor a book).

Step 2 ∎

Work individually.

Arrange to observe a reading lesson. Your trainer will give you a copy of the **Observation table: Classroom reading**. Include at least five examples of reading observed.

Step 3 ∎

Work individually.

After completing the task, answer the Post-observation questions in writing.

Post-observation questions

1 *a* What appeared to be three purposes of people reading in real life (e.g. for information)?
b What appeared to be three purposes of reading English in the classroom (e.g. for pronunciation practice)?

2 *a* How often did someone read aloud in real life compared with reading aloud in the classroom?

b What appeared to be the aim of reading aloud?

c What is your opinion about reading aloud in the classroom?

3 What was the difference between the sort of texts read inside and outside the classroom?

4 How can reading inside the classroom be made to resemble real-life reading (e.g. allow time for reading for entertainment, create a more home-like atmosphere by playing quiet background music)?

5 What can a teacher do to make the aims of reading clear to her learners (e.g. She can say, *Today we're going to...*)?

6 What are some possible ways to motivate learners to read English and to enjoy reading?

Reflection

TASK 2 The tortoise or the hare?

In this task you decide which reading strategies you believe are effective or ineffective when you read in a foreign language and then you identify which reading strategies you use.

Step 1 **P**

Work in pairs.

1 Your trainer will give you a copy of the table **Which reading strategies are effective?** Discuss the reading strategies (a–v). Think about reading in a foreign language. In the middle column, if you think the strategy is effective, write an *E*; if you think the strategy is ineffective, write an *I*.

2 In the right-hand column, note down the reason(s) for your opinions. One example is done for you.

Step 2 **G**

Work in groups.

Discuss these questions:

1 Do you agree about which are effective and ineffective reading strategies?

2 How many of the effective strategies do you use when you read in a foreign language?

3 How many of them do you use when you read in your own language?

4 *a* Having done this task, do you think you are efficient readers in a foreign language?

b Why or why not?

5 *a* Which of these effective reading strategies are new to you?

b Which of these would like to try out? Why?

6 *a* Do any of the members of your group use the same ineffective strategies when reading in a foreign language?

b If these ineffective strategies are commonly encouraged in your country, what is the teacher's apparent aim in using them?

Reading

TASK 3 Browsing...

This task introduces you to different ways of teaching reading.

Step 1

Work individually.

Read the quotes from experienced teachers around the world. As you read, underline any new ideas about teaching reading that appeal to you.

I like to use English language newspaper or magazine articles with all of my learners some of the time. My colleagues ask me, 'How can you do that with beginning readers? I can't!' I think they imagine that I ask my learners to sit down and read a whole article, which I never do. In fact, I only use selected parts of the articles from the paper. Sometimes I just ask them to match headlines to pictures, other times to find three words in an advertisement describing a product. Or they might scan for the name of the country that an article was written about. These are pretty simple tasks, but the learners seem to like knowing that they can understand parts of a real English-language newspaper.

Juana

Invariably, when I give my learners a text to read, I first ask them to read it once very quickly for the main ideas. Once everyone has got the general idea, they read the whole passage again, then one or two of them tell me in their own words what they understood. Next, I usually ask them to work in pairs or small groups to find answers to more detailed questions: they always read the passage at least twice more to scan and find the answers. By doing it like this, I think they get a lot more out of the text, and there's plenty of learner-to-learner interaction, too.

Britt

I discourage the use of dictionaries in the classroom: learners can become over-dependent on them. I try to get my learners to guess words that they don't know, or if they can't manage that, then I try to help them to find out the meaning by asking leading questions. If they really don't understand something, they can look it up in their dictionaries at home.

Astrid

I've been teaching for ten years and in my reading lessons I always go around the class, asking individual learners to read aloud in turn. In this way, the other learners understand clearly: they can hear something as they follow in their books and I can also check their pronunciation. They seem to like being the ones to 'shine' — at least, when they pronounce the sentences correctly!

Ahmed

When I teach reading, I give the learners the text to read and ask them to read it aloud, one by one. Then we go over any unfamiliar vocabulary, when I try to have learners guess the meaning. If they can't, I give them the equivalent word in their native language. Then I ask them a couple of basic questions to check their comprehension of the main ideas. After that learners work in pairs to answer comprehension questions and then we re-assemble into one class and check all the answers.

Xu

A lot of teachers I have worked with often ask their learners to read aloud. When a learner reads aloud, he often feels tense, and that can't really help him to grasp new language, can it? Besides, after he's read aloud, he usually can't even answer a basic question: he has to reread the passage silently to try to find the answer. So I don't think it's helpful at all and I don't do it any more. I wish more of my colleagues agreed!

Annemarie

I always give my class the activity that they are to do at the same time as I give out the text; I never ask them just to 'read the text' because they wouldn't have a reason, then, to read. So I explain the activity and then they can do it while they are reading.

— *Orlando*

When I teach reading, I like my learners to use the other skills, too. I do various things. For example, before reading a passage, my learners discuss the topic or brainstorm vocabulary they predict they will hear; or they listen to a short passage on a related topic and discuss it. At the reading stage, I make sure to spell out why they are reading. We read a passage more than once, each time with a new task. The learners fill in a chart, or match pictures to paragraphs or answer true/false questions. Finally, I save enough time for a follow-up, like a role-play or group work where the learners write a different ending or discuss the issue in the text.

— *Kate*

When I prepare to teach a reading passage, I read it once or twice and underline essential words that the learners might not know. I circle the words which might be similar to the learners' first language or which might be easily explained by the context surrounding the word; I then decide how many of the remaining underlined words to pre-teach. I only pre-teach a few new key words — maybe five in a passage that's two or three paragraphs long — because I don't want my learners relying on me for every single definition. With the circled words, I often write the sentences in which they occur on the board and the learners work in small groups to guess the meaning from the context. After they've read the text, I often do an activity, such as a role-play or a game, to practise the new vocabulary they have come across.

— *Liu*

In my intermediate-level class, I try to get my learners to read as much English as possible; the only way learners will really become good readers is by reading. We have assembled an attractive-looking English reading shelf in the classroom, collecting as much interesting information as possible, such as teenage magazines or articles that we've taken from newspapers or course books. I don't make the learners read anything specific, but they have to choose and read three passages in a week and keep a log of what they've written. In the log, I just ask them to write a couple of sentences about what they found interesting about each text they read. After all, their ideas really matter.

— *Isabella*

Step 2

Work in pairs. Answer the Focus questions.

Focus questions

1 *a* Identify four pre-reading activities from the quotes.
   b What are the aims of each one?

2 *a* On the topic of reading aloud, which teacher do you most agree with, Ahmed or Annemarie?
   b What is the aim of reading aloud?
   c Do you think reading aloud is effective?
   d Why/why not?

3 *a* Kate and Xu's quotes outline two different models for teaching a reading lesson. Briefly outline these two models.
   b What is one advantage and one disadvantage of each of these models?

4 *a* Several of these teachers give their students activities to do as they are reading. Why do they do this?
   b Do you like this way of teaching reading? Why/why not?

5 Why does Britt advocate reading for the main ideas before reading for details?

6 *a* Identify five post-reading activities from the quotes which students do after they have understood the text.
   b What is the aim of each one?

TASK 4 Reader's choice   **P**

In this task you match different reading techniques with reading activities from coursebooks.

Work in pairs.

1 Read the descriptions of reading techniques (1–12) in the table below.

2 Look at the reading activities (A–K) on pages 63-65. Which reading techniques do they practise? Write the corresponding letter of each reading activity (A-K) in the right-hand column of the table. Two examples have been done for you.

Reading techniques and their purposes		
Reading technique	**Description and purpose**	**Activity**
1 Skimming	Reading a passage quickly to grasp the main idea (or gist).	
2 Scanning	Reading a passage quickly to find specific information.	
3 Contextual guessing	Making guesses about the meaning of words by looking at the surrounding words or situation.	
4 Cloze exercise	Fill-in-the-blank exercise, in which some words are omitted, designed to measure how well the reader understands how a text is linked together.	
5 Outlining	Note-taking technique designed to help the reader see the overall organisation of a text.	
6 Paraphrasing	The ability to say or write ideas in other words; measures the reader's understanding of the main ideas of a text.	*A, E*
7 Scrambled stories	Also known as 'jigsaw reading': the reader re-orders the mixed up pieces of a text to show he understands how a text fits together.	
8 Information transfer	Exercise which requires readers to transfer information from the text into another form of related text or drawing (e.g. filling in a chart, tracing a route on a map); designed to measure comprehension.	
9 Making inferences	'Reading between the lines': the reader understands what is meant but not stated in a passage.	
10 Intensive reading	Reading carefully for *complete*, detailed comprehension, (e.g. main ideas, details, vocabulary).	
11 Extensive reading	Reading widely in order to improve reading comprehension, reading speed and vocabulary.	*A*
12 Passage completion	Finishing a reading passage (orally or in writing); involves predicting a logical or suitable conclusion based on a thorough understanding of the text.	

READING ACTIVITIES A–K

Reading activity A

Read another short story of your choice. Write a journal entry summarising the main points of the plot.

Reading activity B

Read the story and decide how it should end. What happens next? Write a conclusion.

Reading activity C

Read the first part of the story. What do you think these words mean?

clever   create   living   dead   experiment   successful

Adapted from *Fountain Beginners*

Reading activity D

Read the text and answer the questions.

Ladies and gentlemen! Behind this screen there are three bottles. One bottle is red, one bottle is blue, and one bottle is green. In one bottle there's water. In one bottle there's milk. And in one bottle there's Coca-Cola.

on the left   in the middle   on the right

Can you find the Coca-Cola? Is it on the left, in the middle, or on the right? Read the clues and find the answer.

Clues

1 The blue bottle is between the red bottle and the bottle of water.
2 The green bottle is next to the bottle of milk.
3 The red bottle is on the left.

Taken from *Mosaic 1*

Reading activity E

Dialogue

Man: I've lost my dog.
Lottie: What does it look like?
Man: What do you mean – 'it'? My dog is a 'she'.
Lottie: Oh, sorry. What does she look like?
Man: Well, she's got four legs...
Lottie: Really?
Man: Yes. She's quite big, and she's white with brown eyes.
Lottie: How big is she?
Man: Well, quite big, not very big. She's about this big. And she looks a bit like me.
Lottie: Like you?

Read the dialogue again. Which sentences mean the same as these?

1 Please describe it.
2 Please describe her.
3 My dog is female.
4 Please describe the dog's size.
5 Look! This is her size.
6 The dog's face and my face are not very different.

Taken from *Mosaic 2*

Reading activity F

Match the instructions with the pictures. The pictures are in the correct order; the instructions aren't.

Instructions

1 Cut the neck off the balloon.
2 Put the bottle into the bowl.
3 Wait for two or three minutes.
4 Pull the balloon over the top of the bottle.
5 Watch carefully.

Taken from *Mosaic 1*

Reading activity G

Now work with a friend. Read the compositions and match these titles to them.
One composition hasn't got a title – can you think of a good one?

Transport
Books
Money
Houses
Politics
Education

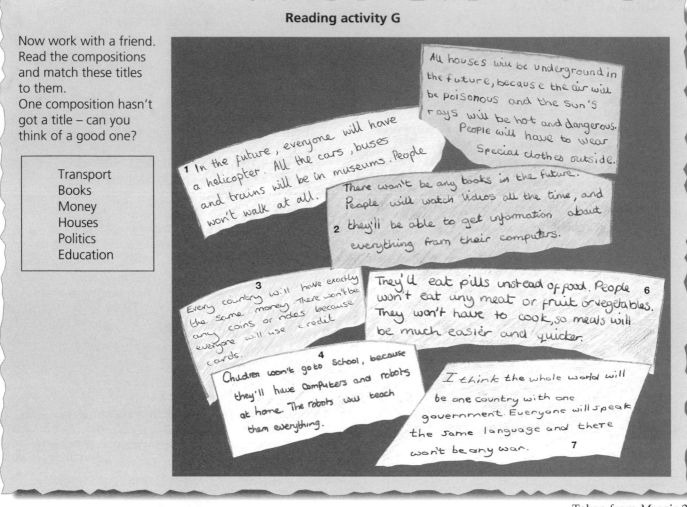

1 In the future, everyone will have a helicopter. All the cars, buses and trains will be in museums. People won't walk at all.

All houses will be underground in the future, because the air will be poisonous and the sun's rays will be hot and dangerous. People will have to wear special clothes outside.

2 There won't be any books in the future. People will watch videos all the time, and they'll be able to get information about everything from their computers.

3 Every country will have exactly the same money. There won't be any coins or notes because everyone will use credit cards.

They'll eat pills instead of food. People **6** won't eat any meat or fruit or vegetables. They won't have to cook, so meals will be much easier and quicker.

4 Children won't go to school, because they'll have computers and robots at home. The robots will teach them everything.

I think the whole world will be one country with one government. Everyone will speak the same language and there won't be any war. **7**

Taken from *Mosaic 2*

Reading activity H

The Nootka lived near the sea. They made canoes from trees. When the Nootka went fishing they used the canoes. They fished either close to the coast or out at sea.

1. What did the Nootka eat?
2. How did they get their food?

Adapted from *At First Sight*

Reading activity I

Read the story and fill in the blanks. There is one missing word for each blank.

I used to live in Turkey. While I was _____, I studied Turkish folk _____ and music. There is a great tradition of dance and _____ in this country – in fact, there are thousands of _____ dances one can learn. The _____ learn many of the basic ones in school and at weddings and other _____. There are different dances for each region of the country, and each _____ has its own costumes, too.

Reading activity J

Read the following passage about earthquakes, then complete the following outline by adding information to each of the points listed in it:

I   Devastating Power of Earthquakes

   A Examples of Great Quakes

      1

      2

      3

   B Richter scale of measurement

II Causes of Earthquakes

   A Previous theories:

      1

      2

      3

   B Currently accepted theory:

Reading activity K

Look quickly at the text and answer the question.

1   Who is the text about?

He was born in 1451.
He lived in Genoa in Italy.
In 1476 he went to Portugal and asked the King for money.
The King said, 'No!' Then he went to Spain.
In Spain King Ferdinand and Queen Isabella gave him men, money, and three ships. The ships were called the *Santa Maria*, the *Nina* and the *Pinta*.
On 3rd August 1492 he sailed from Palos in Spain.
He stopped in the Canary Islands. Then he sailed across the Atlantic.
He landed in the Bahamas on 12th October 1492.
He thought he was in Asia.
He sailed to Cuba and to Hispaniola.
He sailed back to Spain in the *Nina*.
He died in 1506.

Taken from *Mosaic 1*

Time out, take five

Journal entry
My favourite reading tasks

Think back about the types of reading tasks you have read about or experienced in this unit. Which of these do you prefer? Why? If you teach now, which ones are best for your students? Explain.

A reading lesson

TASK 5 Upside down, inside out

In this task you re-order a mixed-up reading lesson which includes pre-reading, while-reading and post-reading. You then plan a reading lesson of your own.

Step 1   G

Work in a group.

1 Together, re-order the reading lesson provided by your trainer. The reading passage for this lesson is entitled *'Fads and Trends in the USA'* (not reproduced here). Be ready to tell the rest of your class why you arranged the lesson in this order.

2 Which of the stages of this lesson are:

a pre-reading activities?
b while-reading activities?
c post-reading activities?

Step 2   G

Work in groups.

1 Find a reading passage that you would like to teach.

2 Write an outline of a reading lesson of your own. Make sure the following is covered in your outline:

- three stages: pre-reading, while-reading and post-reading
- the specific aims of each activity
- logical transitions from one stage of the lesson to the next.

3 Share your lesson outlines with other groups or give them to your trainer to look at.

Microteaching

TASK 6 You can't judge a book by its cover

In this task, you teach or are taught a reading activity. If you are new to microteaching, read **3. Microteaching tasks** and **4. Feedback questions** on pages v-vi of the introduction.

Step 1 **P**

Work in pairs.

Prepare the following:

1 Select a *short* reading passage (maximum length of 150 words) to teach to your class: find a passage in a coursebook or some authentic material.

2 Devise a ten-minute *while-reading* activity to use with this text. (For inspiration, look back at other tasks in this unit.) Be clear yourself about the aim(s) of your activity.

3 As you design your reading activity, think through the Feedback questions in Step 2, which will be discussed after the microteaching.

Step 2 **G**

Work in groups of 6 or 8.

1 Decide upon your roles. Either teach your while-reading activity, or experience one as if you were a learner.

2 Give feedback to the teacher(s) involved in leading the activity by discussing the Feedback questions.

Feedback questions

1 Did the teacher(s) motivate you to want to read?

2 How effectively did the activity help you to comprehend the entire reading text?

3 How would you improve the activity?

4 Which reading skills were practised?

5 Are the reading skills in the activity useful in real life?

6 Any further comments on the teaching?

Game

TASK 7 If the shoe doesn't fit... **G**

In this game, you 'think on your feet,' making decisions in order to suggest solutions to a variety of common situations that may arise while teaching reading.

Instructions:

1 Sit in threes around a table. Place a set of **Situation cards** (from your trainer) face down in the middle of the table.

2 The first player draws a **Situation card**. He reads the situation on the card aloud to the rest of the group, then describes what he would do to solve that problem. The others in the circle listen and either approve or disapprove of the suggestion; if they approve, the first player gets a point. If not, he has to pass, putting the card at the bottom of the pile; the next person draws a new card and takes his turn.

3 Continue until all the **Situation cards** have been used or a time limit has been called. The winner is the person with the most points.

Further reading

Carrell, Patricia L., Joanne Devine and David Eskey, eds. 1988. *Interactive Approaches to Second Language Reading.* Cambridge: Cambridge University Press.
    Selected articles on recent research and theory into reading as an interactive process between the text and reader.

Day, Richard, ed. 1993. *New Ways in Teaching Reading.* Alexandria, VA: TESOL.
    An anthology of recipes to teach reading for diverse levels and purposes.

Frederickson, Terry L. and Paul F. Wedel. 1984. *English by Newspaper.* Boston: Heinle and Heinle.
    Texts for advanced readers.

Grellet, Françoise. 1981. *Developing Reading Skills.* Cambridge: Cambridge University Press.
    A thoughtful analysis of reading skills with suggested activities for how to use them.

Grundy, Peter. 1993. *Newspapers.* Oxford: Oxford University Press.
    Ideas for creating your own activities using newspapers.

Hadfield, Jill and Charles. 1995. *Reading Games.* Harlow: Addison Wesley Longman
    A collection of reading games and activities for intermediate to advanced learners.

Hess, Natalie. 1991. *Headstarts.* Harlow: Pilgrims-Addison Wesley Longman.
    A hundred activities for pre-reading.

Holme, Randall. 1991. *Talking Texts.* Harlow: Pilgrims-Addison Wesley Longman.
    Lots of ideas for intensive reading tasks.

Kirn, Elaine and Pamela Hartmann. 1985. *Interactions II: A Reading Skills Book.* Second edition. New York: McGraw-Hill, Inc.
    A reading text based on skills development for the low-intermediate learner.

Lazar, Gillian. 1987. *Literature in the Language Classroom.* Cambridge: Cambridge University Press.
    Contains a series of activities (with key) designed to encourage reflection on issues in using literature to teach language.

Nuttall, Christine. 1996. *Teaching Reading Skills in a Foreign Language.* Oxford: Heinemann.
    A new edition of a classic book on all aspects of teaching reading.

Sokolik, Margaret E. 1993. *Global Views: Readings about World Issues.* Boston: Heinle and Heinle.
    An advanced reading textbook focusing on global citizenship, with exercises to encourage reflection and comprehension.

9 DEAR DIARY

Teaching writing

Writing

TASK 1 To whom it may concern

In this task you experience and compare two approaches to writing.

Step 1

1 Divide into two groups, A and B.

2 Individually, do the writing assignment that corresponds to your letter, which will be provided by your trainer. You must finish it in 30 minutes.

Step 2

Pair up with another person from your group, A or B, and discuss the Focus questions below.

Focus questions

1 What was the aim of your writing assignment?

2 Who was your intended audience?

3 How did your assignment help you prepare to write?

4 How would you improve the assignment provided?

Step 3

Form groups of four: two As and two Bs. The As read Bs' writing, and the Bs read As' writing. Next, discuss the Focus questions below with your group.

Focus questions

1 Describe your assignments. Find at least two main differences between the two writing activities.

2 How did the stages of your assignment help or hinder your writing?

3 What are two strengths and two weaknesses of each assignment, A and B?

4 Which approach to writing do you prefer? Why?

TASK 2 Putting pen to paper

In this task you experience group writing, then analyse its advantages and disadvantages.

Step 1

Work in groups.

Imagine you are a team of journalists and that you are going to write a description of a vacation spot for a travel magazine.

1 Look at your picture of a holiday destination (your trainer will provide this). Complete these sentence stems with several different words and phrases you might use to liven up your article:

a We can see...
b We can smell...
c We can hear...

2 Together, write a short paragraph (about five sentences), describing your vacation spot in a catchy way and incorporating some of the words and phrases that you like from your notes.
Limit your time to ten minutes. Note: others in the class will be asked to match your picture with your

description, so don't be too obvious or too obscure when you write.

3 Display your paragraphs and pictures separately and then match the pictures to the descriptions.

Step 2

Work in new groups.

Discuss these Focus questions.

Focus questions

1 What was the purpose of each stage in Step 1?

2 How did the pre-writing activity (question 1) help you to write?

3 What would be a logical activity to do after the writing activity is finished?

4 What did you enjoy about writing in a group? Write down three advantages of group writing.

5 What did you NOT like about writing in a group? Write down some possible disadvantages.

6 Think of two examples of group writing that occur in real life. What are the aims of the real-life group writing?

....

Analysing writing activities

TASK 3 Doodling

Writing activities are sometimes incomplete or do not give our learners the practice they need. In this task you analyse several writing activities and suggest pre- and post-writing activities for some of them.

Step 1 P

Work in pairs.

1 What did you write in your own language in the last 48 hours? Make one list for the two of you.

2 Look at your list. For three of your items, tell each other the following:

a the aim (e.g. to remind, to apologise, to inform)

b the audience (i.e. the person who read the item)

c the *genre*, or text type (e.g. shopping list, personal letter, registration form).

3 Do we always have an aim, audience and genre when we write in 'real life'?

Step 2

Work in groups.

On pages 71–2 are six examples of writing activities (A–F) from coursebooks. Identify four different characteristics for each writing activity:

a aim
b audience
c genre
d level (beginner, intermediate, etc.)

Note: Some activities may already be suited to more than one genre or level. For others there may be some missing elements. An example is done for you.

Example:

Write a one-page magazine advertisement for a washing machine your company produces, called WHIRLCLEAN.

a aim: not specified (implied aim is to sell a washing machine to a prospective customer)
b audience: a potential customer
c genre: a one-page ad
d level: intermediate to advanced

Writing activity A

Rosie's school report

Look at Rosie's school report. Write your own school report for the year. Explain how well you have done in each subject. Your parents will read it.

GRIMCASTLE SCHOOL   Summer term

Name: Rosie   **Surname:** Malone   **Age:** 14   **Class:** 2B

Subject	Mark	Comments	Teacher
Art	B	Good. Rosie likes this subject and is very interested in Art. She has worked very hard and she has drawn some very nice pictures this year.	MM
English	C	Average. Rosie quite likes this subject, but she must listen in class. She has worked quite hard and she has written some good stories, but her spelling isn't very good.	PW
French	E	Very weak. Rosie doesn't like this subject at all. She hasn't worked very hard. Her spelling is very bad and her vocabulary is very small. She sometimes eats in class.	R.C.
Geography	D	Weak. Rosie doesn't like this subject at all and finds it difficult. She occasionally goes to sleep in class. Her writing is very untidy.	D.L.
History	B	Good. Rosie likes this subject very much and she has worked quite hard. She has an excellent memory.	A.P.
Latin	A	Excellent. Rosie's exam was the best in the class. I was surprised because she hasn't worked very hard and she doesn't like this subject.	J.C.
Maths	A	Excellent, Rosie's Maths has improved tremendously this year. She has worked very hard and she is now one of the best students in the class. But why does she write her answers in Roman numerals?	
Music	D	Weak. Rosie isn't interested in this subject and she hasn't worked very hard. She's often late for class and she only does her homework occasionally.	WH
Science	E	Very weak. Rosie doesn't like Science at all and she hasn't worked very hard. In fact, she hasn't worked at all. She sometimes talks in class and she never listens.	I.N.
Sport	C	Average. Rosie likes sport and she can run fast. She has worked quite hard, but she isn't interested in tennis.	BB

Taken from *Fountain Elementary*

Writing activity B

Look at these advertisements. Choose one and write a letter asking for further information.

LEISURELY CYCLING
in beautiful English Lakeland as seen on T.V. Choice of good Hotels, Guest Homes. 7 day price choice from £126/260. 'All luggage transported.' Free days. Highly recom. for all age groups. Col. Broch.
CYCLORAMA HOLIDAYS
GRANGE HOTEL
Grange-over-Sands (1),
Cumbria, LA11 6EJ
Tel: (04484) 3666.

TENNIS HOLIDAYS
Weekends/5 days/7 days. Expert coaching / play. 18 outdoor/indoor courts. Full accom. Heated pool. 9 hole par 3 golf course. 20 lovely acres. Near Eastbourne/sea. Col. Broch.
Windmill Hill Place Tennis Resort, Dept O, Hailsham, E. Sussex.
(0323) 832552

Taken from *Mode 2*

Writing activity C

Write a paragraph to describe Mary Shelley from the point of view of her husband. Mary's daughter will read it.

Writing activity D

Imagine Saturday is going to be a perfect day. What are you going to do? What aren't you going to do? Write a letter for your friend to read. Invite her/him to join you in your activities.

Writing activity E

Write your own radio advertisement for a European Cities tour. Encourage other learners your age to join the tour.

GATEWAY · HOLIDAYS ● LONDON
European Cities Tours

Our basic tour:
TRAVEL by ferry and coach.
VISIT France, Germany and Holland.
SEE the Eiffel Tower, Cologne Cathedral and Anne Frank's house.
STAY in hostels and one-star hotels.
NUMBER OF DAYS: 5 **COST:** £99

Our deluxe tour:
TRAVEL by plane and train.
VISIT Portugal, Italy, Greece, Turkey, Austria and France.
SEE the Alfama, the Leaning Tower of Pisa, the Acropolis, St Sophia, the Big Wheel and the Arc de Triomphe.
STAY in five-star hotels.
NUMBER OF DAYS: 14 **COST:** £850

Taken from
Fountain Elementary

Writing activity F

Write a paragraph that describes teenagers from different countries. Your description may appear in a magazine for teenagers.

Step 3   **G**

Work in groups.

1 Pre-writing

Choose one of the writing activities in Step 2. What would you do to prepare your learners for writing? For more guidance, look back at writing assignment B in **Task 2 Putting pen to paper** (p. 70) and also **Task 5 Paving the way** (p. 38) from **Unit 5 Warming up**.

Think about:
a introducing the topic of your writing activity
b introducing helpful language
c interesting learners in the topic.

2 Post-writing

Once your learners have completed their writing activity, what could they do to consolidate and perhaps practise the language they used while writing? Design a post-writing activity for your learners, practising another skill (e.g. speaking).

TASK 4 A stroke of the pen

In this task you adapt writing activities from coursebooks to make them more communicative, i.e. you give each activity a realistic aim, audience and genre.

Step 1   **P**

Work in pairs.

1 Read these two writing activities from coursebooks:

> ### Writing activity A: A composition
>
> Write a short composition on one of these topics. Discuss the advantages and disadvantages.
>
> Study holidays
>
> Living in a large family
>
> Nuclear power
>
> Make sure you write four paragraphs ... and use some of the language suggested [in the unit] for each paragraph.

Adapted from *Mode 2*

> ### Writing activity B: A school sports day
>
> Write about a school sports day. Then read it carefully. Are there any mistakes? Give it to a friend to check.

Taken from *Mosaic 1*

2 Neither of these writing activities include a clear aim, an audience or a genre. Rewrite each activity so that it includes:

a an aim

b an audience

c a genre.

In this way, you are making the activities communicative, that is making them resemble written communication in real life. You might have to change the activities quite a lot, but try to keep them at the same level and to include the same language that is implied by the original activities.

Step 2   **P**

Work in pairs.

Read the new activities created by at least five other pairs. Discuss which you like best and why.

Time out, take five

> *Journal entry*
> ## Where do I stand now?
>
> How well prepared do you feel to teach writing activities? What would you enjoy most about teaching writing? What do you still want to learn about teaching writing?

Microteaching

TASK 5 Take note

In this task, you design and teach or are taught a pre-writing or post-writing activity. If you are new to microteaching, read **3. Microteaching tasks** and **4. Feedback questions** on pages v–vi of the introduction.

Step 1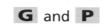

1 Work in groups of four. Read the following writing activity.

> Write your own recipe for a sandwich. You can invent an unusual one if you like. Remember to include:
> - ingredients
> - equipment
> - instructions

Taken from *World Class 2*

Write down the aim, audience, genre and level of the writing activity.

2 Divide into two pairs.

a One pair designs and prepares to teach a five-minute pre-writing activity for the writing assignment. Clarify who is going to teach what and in which order.

b The other pair designs and prepares to teach a five-minute post-writing activity. Clarify who is going to teach what and in which order.

Step 2

You will either work with a partner to teach one stage of a writing activity, or you will experience one as if you were a learner. After each micro-lesson has been taught, give feedback to the teachers. Use the following Feedback questions as a guide.

Feedback questions

1 How did the pre-writing activity prepare you for the activity?

2 How did the post-writing activity complete the lesson?

3 How would you do the pre- and post-writing activities differently?

4 Any additional comments on the teaching?

Game

TASK 6 Writer's block

Typically learners experience a number of problems when writing. In this game, you match possible solutions to typical problems that learners face when learning to write in English.

Work in groups.

Materials:

Your trainer will provide:
one set of **Problem cards** per group;
one set of **Solution cards** per group.

Instructions:

1 Sit in groups around tables. Appoint a person to keep score.

2 Deal out the **Solution cards** and put the **Problem cards** on the table, face down.

3 The first player draws one **Problem card** and reads it aloud. The person who thinks he has matching solution should read it aloud. The rest of the players listen to the proposed solution and accept or reject it. If everyone agrees it is a good solution and no one has a better one in his hand, the person with the **Solution card** receives one point. If someone else proposes a better solution from his hand and the group accepts it, he gets the point. The person receiving the point keeps the matching **Problem card**.

4 If you draw a **Wild card**, invent your own problem or solution. Try to create situations you really expect to encounter in your teaching context.

5 The game continues until all the problems have been solved or time is called. The winner is the player with the highest score.

Further reading

Greuber, Diann and Dunn, Viviane. 1987. *Writing Elementary*. Oxford: Oxford University Press.
  Task-based activities for writing.

Boutin, Marie-Christine, Suzanne Brinand and Francoise Grellet. 1987. *Writing Intermediate*. Oxford: Oxford University Press.
  Task-based activities for writing.

Hadfield, Charles and Jill Hadfield. 1990. *Writing Games*. Harlow: Addison Wesley Longman.
  Writing games and creative activities for low-intermediate to advanced learners.

Hedge, Tricia. 1988. *Writing*. Oxford: Oxford University Press.
  Contains a wide variety of writing activities for all levels and numerous purposes.

Hill, David A. 1990. *Visual Impact*. Harlow: Pilgrims-Addison Wesley Longman.
  Creative language learning activities using pictures.

Maley, Alan and Alan Duff. 1989. *The Inward Ear: Poetry in the Language Classroom*. Cambridge: Cambridge University Press.
  Using poetry in the classroom to develop learners' writing of poetry.

Nolasco, Rob. 1987. *Writing Upper-Intermediate*. Oxford: Oxford University Press.
  Task-based activities for writing.

Nunan, David. 1995. 'Chapter Five, Developing Writing Skills' in *Language Teaching Methodology: A Textbook for Teachers*. Hemel Hempstead: Phoenix ELT.
  Surveys recent literature and includes insightful perspectives on theory of teaching writing.

Peyton, Joy Kreeft and Leslee Reed. 1990. *Dialogue Journal Writing with Non-native English Speakers: A Handbook for Teachers*. Alexandria, VA: TESOL.
  Practical guide for using journal writing in the ESL/EFL classroom.

Peyton, Joy Kreeft, ed. 1990. *Learners and Teachers Writing Together: Perspectives on Journal Writing*. Alexandria, VA: TESOL.
  Selected articles on the role of journal writing in language development.

Raimes, Anne. 1983. *Techniques in Teaching Writing*. Oxford: Oxford University Press.
  Addresses complex theoretical issues in simple English and includes practical techniques for teaching writing at multiple levels.

White, Ron. 1987. *Writing Advanced*. Oxford: Oxford University Press.
  Task-based activities for writing.

Woolcott, Lyn. 1992. *Take Your Pick*. Harlow: Addison Wesley Longman.
  Activities for using photographs in language learning, including sets of photos provided.

10 PUTTING IT ALL TOGETHER
Integrating the skills

Reflection

TASK 1 Warp and weft

In this task you reflect on how language skills are interwoven in real life.

Step 1

Work in pairs.

Use the table on the next page. Match one event in the **Initial events** column with the event that would best come after it in the **Following events** column. Note: not all the **Following events** will match the **Initial events**. One example is done for you.

Step 2

Work in pairs.

Imagine a classroom activity in which the learners listen to a conversation among four people talking about plans for a New Year's Eve party.

1 What might be an appropriate (i.e. like real life) follow-on activity to do in class, using a different language skill?

2 What might be an appropriate activity to do in class before the activity, using a different language skill?

INITIAL EVENTS	FOLLOWING EVENTS
a) Read with horror a very high gas bill.	1 Called to speak to a babysitter.
b) Listened to a message on the answering machine; wife explained that she is bringing her boss home for dinner tonight.	2 Read about her problem in a medical textbook.
c) Wrote a note to a colleague, requesting a meeting to discuss a problem.	3 Listened to her proposed solutions face to face.
d) Spoke to a learner about his absence.	4 Wrote a card to accompany the flowers.
e) Listened to a friend's medical problem.	5 Read a doctor's excuse the learner gave me.
f) Phoned in an order to send flowers for Grandma's 70th birthday.	6 Rang another family member to tell them the news.
g) Heard some family news on the telephone.	7 Spoke to the gas company representative by phone.
h) Received a printed invitation to a fancy dress party next Saturday.	8 Wrote a letter to address the problem.
	9 Read some recipes for quick gourmet dinners.
	10 Read about a new policy in the newspaper.

An integrated skills lesson

TASK 2 In unison

In this task you re-order the stages of an integrated skills lesson. This one is based on a coursebook for teenage beginners.

Step 1 **P**

Work in pairs.

Your trainer will provide a mixed-up lesson plan. Put the stages of the lesson plan (a–i) in a logical order.

Step 2 **G**

Join another pair of trainees and agree on a joint plan. Discuss the Focus questions.

Focus questions

1 *a* What is another possible order for this lesson?
  b How might a different order affect learners' learning?

2 What do you think of the balance of the skills in this lesson?

3 Which parts would you most enjoy teaching and why?

4 What might be a logical follow-on to this lesson?

5 How is this lesson similar to or different from lessons in your teaching context?

TASK 3 There's a song in my heart   Work in groups.

In this task you analyse an integrated skills lesson based on a song.

Read the lesson plan below and the materials accompanying the lesson on the next page. Then discuss the Focus questions.

Lesson plan: Integrating the skills based on a song

Aims:

- To listen for the main idea of a text and for specific information
- To guess vocabulary from context and learn new vocabulary
- To discuss reactions to the lyrics of a song
- To write a letter to a penfriend
- To develop critical thinking skills (making inferences, analysing)
- To foster learner independence and cooperative learning.

Materials:

- Recording of song 'Why?' by Tracy Chapman (1986)
- Copies of Cloze exercise 'Why?' by Tracy Chapman
- Copies of Matching opposites exercise
- Copies of Writing task
- Cassette recorder

Stages of the Lesson:

1   Warm up (5 min): Tell Ls they are going to work on a song today. Give out Matching Opposites exercise to pairs of learners. Ls complete in 3 min. Tell Ls that many of these words are taken from the song.

   Whole class brainstorms the topic of the song and, possibly, the singer's name (2 min).

2   Give out song with gaps; play song once or twice, depending on Ls' needs. Learners fill in blanks while listening, then check in pairs.

3   Ls check answers on overhead projector (5-10 min)

   Answer key to cloze exercise:
   1) alone; 2) peace; 3) safe; 4) love; 5) war; 6) free; 7) answer; 8) truth; 9) answer; 10) blind

4   (5 min). Write sentences a–c on board and ask class which sentence best summarises the song:
   (a) There is a lot of injustice in the world and something must be done.
   (b) There are many lonely people in the world and they should be helped.
   (c) Poor people have a right to the same job as rich people.

5   Ask whole class what words they don't understand; elicit answers from other Ls as far as possible; help with problems (5 min).

6   Ls work in 4s. Discuss (a) what emotions the person in the song feels and (b) why they believe this (5 min).

7   Give Ls individual Writing task; check that Ls understand; Ls begin in class and finish for homework.

8   Re-cap homework (2 min): finish writing the letter. Tell Ls to be prepared to show it to others in class during the next lesson.

Materials accompanying the Lesson plan

Matching opposites

Match the words in the left column with their opposites (or near-opposites) in the right column. One example is done for you.

a) love	1	death
b) life	2	enslaved
c) safe	3	question
d) together	4	hate
e) peace	5	injustice
f) truth	6	in danger
g) answer	7	alone
h) sighted	8	war
i) justice	9	blind
j) free	10	falsehood

Writing task

Imagine your American penfriend is the person in this song. She is feeling bad and has written the song 'Why?'. She sent you a copy of the lyrics and asks you for help. You want to try to help her have more hope about the future. In your letter, put your friend's ideas into your own words to show that you understand her feelings.

Cloze exercise: 'Why?' by Tracy Chapman

[CHORUS = lines 1–12]

1 Why do the babies starve
When there's enough feed the world
Why when there're so many of us
Are there people still 1) _____

5 Why are the missiles called 2) _____ keepers
When they're aimed to kill
Why is a woman still not 3) _____
When she's in her home

9 4) _____ is hate
5) _____ is peace
No is yes
And we're all 6) _____

13 But somebody's gonna to have to 7) _____
The time is coming soon
Amidst all these questions and contradictions
There're some who seek the 8) _____

[CHORUS]

17 But somebody's gonna to have to 9) _____
The time is coming soon
When the 10) _____ remove their blinders
And the speechless speak the truth

[CHORUS]

Focus questions

1 What level (beginning, intermediate, etc.) is this lesson most suited for? Why?

2 *a* Not all language areas – the four skills, grammar and vocabulary – are practised in this lesson. Which area is not taught?
b What is the effect of omitting it?

3 What are two advantages of using songs for an integrated skills lesson?

4 What might the disadvantages of using songs be?

5 Why is it useful to use the same material to practise different language skills, grammar or vocabulary?

6 Suggest two English songs that you think are suitable for an integrated skills lesson and say why you think they are suitable.

Time out, take five

Journal entry
Which language areas do I prefer?

Which of the language areas do you most like practising in a foreign language and why?

Which of the language areas do you think you will most enjoy teaching? Why?

Integrated skills activities

TASK 4 Kaleidoscope

In this task you examine ten activities to do after reading a passage.

Step 1   **G**

Work in groups.

1 Read the intermediate-level reading text *The flying boat* and the ten Integrated skills activities (A–J) that are based on it.

2 *a* Which two activities does your group like the most?
   b Why?

3 *a* Which two activities do you like the least?
   b Why?

The flying boat

Interviewer: I know you've travelled by flying boat. When was this?

Mrs Carrel: I went by flying boat to Singapore in October 1946. At six in the morning on Wednesday we left Poole Harbour, on the south coast, and we arrived in Singapore at four o'clock in the afternoon on the Saturday. I believe now they do it in about fifteen hours flying time. Of course, it was much more comfortable the way I did it.

Interviewer: Yes, I've heard there was a lot of room in the flying boats. And these days in aeroplanes there isn't.

Mrs Carrel: That's right. It was without doubt the most comfortable journey I've made by air in my life. There was also the advantage of slowly getting used to the change in temperature. It was mid-October when I left England, and it was beginning to get cold. At the other end it was very hot, but we were able to get used to the change very gradually.

Interviewer: Yes, that's a major problem these days with air travel …

Mrs Carrel: Yes, particularly in the winter. You fly out from here and fifteen hours later you're suddenly hot and uncomfortable. But I remember flying over France we were really hot. They had heating in the plane, you see. And outside, I knew it was freezing because I could see ice on the wings. The only time we were really cold was between Rangoon and Singapore. The heating was off and we were all wrapped up in blankets.

Taken from Shades of Meaning

Integrated skills activity A

Vocabulary work   **P** 10 min

Underline five words whose meaning you would like to know. With a partner, look at the surrounding context of each word. What clues about the word's meaning do the surrounding words give you? What part of speech is it (e.g. noun, verb)? Based on your answers, make some guesses about its meaning. Compare your answers by talking to another pair of learners.

Integrated skills activity B

Re-write the interview as a story   **I** 10 min

Individually, tell the story again in the third person singular. Begin writing with 'There once was a woman named Mrs Carrel.'

Integrated skills activity C

Interview another character from the story
                                              P 10 min

Imagine you are talking to the pilot of the flying boat, rather than a passenger. Create an interview with him/her. Practise your interview with a partner.

Integrated skills activity D

Give the story a new title   **G** 5 min

In groups, invent another title for the story, and write sub-headings for each section of the interview.

Integrated skills activity E

Write your own conclusion to the interview
                                              I 5-10 min

Pretend you are Mrs Carrel. On your own, write your answer to the interviewer's last question.

Integrated skills activity F

Retell the story   **C** 10-15 min

With your classmates, take turns being Mrs Carrel. The first person begins the story by mentioning one point that Mrs Carrel said. The next person adds another point and so on until a chain has been formed and everyone has spoken.

Integrated skills activity G

Re-write the story in 1946   **P** 15 min

Work with a partner to change the story from the past to the present. Imagine it is 1946 and Mrs Carrel is being interviewed now while she is a passenger on the flying boat.

Integrated skills activity H

Dramatise the story   **C** 15 min

Imagine you and your classmates are the first passengers ever to fly in the flying boat. Create a role-play. What are you talking about? Where are you going? How does the inside of the plane feel (e.g. warm, cold)? What can you see? Practise this drama, acting it out with your classmates.

Integrated skills activity I

Listen for the differences   **I** and **P** 10 min

Listen to the tape (books closed) and individually write three differences between travelling by flying boat in 1946 and by plane nowadays. Check your answers with a partner.

Integrated skills activity J

Verb hunt   **I** 10 min

On your own, write down all the irregular past tense verbs in the passage. Next to each irregular past tense (e.g. *saw*), write the corresponding past participle (e.g. *seen*).

Step 2   **G**

Form new groups. Discuss your answers to the following questions.

1 What is the aim of each of the activities A–J?

2 *a* Which of the activities might you use for a group of thirty 13-year-olds?
    b In which order would you teach your chosen activities? Why?

Lesson planning and microteaching

TASK 5 A unified vision

In this task you write an integrated skills lesson plan and teach part of it. Examples of such lessons are included in this unit, in **Task 2 In unison** (p. 77) and **Task 3 There's a song in my heart** (pp. 78–79). If you have never written a lesson plan before, you can look at **Unit 13 Plan of attack** [**Task 1 Bits and pieces** (pp. 98–9), and **Task 5 Aim straight** (p. 102)].

Step 1

Work in pairs.

1 Pick a theme around which you can create a 45-minute lesson plan integrating the skills.

Profile of learners

- 30 learners (half boys, half girls)
- Age: 16-17
- Level: Intermediate
- Number of 45-minute English lessons per week: 5

---

2 Select some materials from a general English coursebook (one that covers multiple skills) or some authentic materials and write a lesson plan using those materials. Include the following points in your plan:

- aim(s) of the lesson
- materials
- stages of the lesson (with suggested timing and groupings of learners)
- several different language areas (reading, listening, writing, speaking, grammar, vocabulary).

Step 2

Work in groups.

Exchange plans with another pair. Tell them about two strengths of their lesson plan and suggest two possible improvements.

Step 3   **G**

Work in different groups.

1 Read the lesson plans. Choose two linked activities from one lesson plan which practise at least two different language areas and which you would like to use for microteaching to your class. Your two activities should last a maximum of ten minutes.

2 Decide on two people from your group who will teach. Choose who will teach which stage and prepare your lesson together.

Step 4   **G** and **C** and **M**

1 Work in large groups of 10–12 or as a whole class. Your trainer will clarify who is teaching and who the learners are for the microteaching. If you are new to microteaching, read **3. Microteaching tasks** and **4. Feedback questions** on pages v-vi of the introduction.

2 Give feedback to the teachers who teach the lesson by discussing the Feedback questions.

Feedback questions

1 Were the teachers' instructions clear?

2 What were the aims of the activities? How well did the teachers reach the aims?

3 How were the activities linked? How else might the teachers have linked them?

4 How would you change or improve the lesson?

5 Any other comments on the teaching or the activities?

Further reading

Anderson, J.R. et alia. 1983. *Integrated Skills Reinforcement: Reading, Writing, Speaking and Listening Across the Curriculum.* New York: Addison Wesley Longman.
    Focuses on the integration of skills across the curriculum in an ESL context.

Brinton, Donna, Marguerite Ann Snow and Marjorie Bingham Wesche. 1985. Chapter 3, 'Theme-Based Instruction in the ESL and EFL Contexts,' in *Content-Based Second Language Instruction.* New York: Newbury House.
    A teacher reference examining the theory and practice of integrating skills in thematic lessons.

Brown, H. Douglas et alia. 1991. *Vistas: An Interactive Course in English.* Englewood Cliffs, NJ: Regents/Prentice Hall.
    An integrated skills coursebook for four levels.

Enright, D.S. and M.L. McCloskey. 1988. *Integrating English: Developing English Language and Literacy in the Multilingual Classroom.* Reading, Mass: Addison-Wesley Longman.
    A teacher reference book for ESL and EFL.

Lawley, Jim and Roger Hunt. 1992. *Fountain.* Harlow: Addison Wesley Longman.
    A four-level course for young teenagers, from beginning to intermediate level. Designed for large, mixed ability classes in secondary schools.

Radley, Paul and Chris Millerchip. 1990. *Mode 1, 2 and 3.* Harlow: Addison Wesley Longman.
    A three-level course, from beginner to intermediate level, designed to appeal to teens and young adults.

Richards, Jack C. with Jonathan Hull and Susan Proctor. 1991. *Interchange: English for International Communication.* Cambridge: Cambridge University Press.
    A three-level coursebook for adults and young adults.

Soars, John and Liz. 1987. *Headway (Intermediate and Upper-Intermediate).* Oxford: Oxford University Press.
    Coursebooks integrating listening, speaking, reading, writing, grammar and vocabulary.

11 RIGHT ON!

Responding to learners' writing

MAP OF UNIT

REFLECTION
Task 1: 'Responding' means...
Defining a teacher's response to learners' writing

Task 2: Taking the plunge
Responding to a piece of writing and reflecting on your response

RESPONDING
Task 3: If u kn rd ths...
Using symbols to give writers feedback

Task 4: A bird's eye view
Examining the overall organisation of a piece of writing

Task 5: Tips from teachers
Looking at how different teachers handle errors in learners' writing

Task 6: Bravo!
Commenting on the strengths of a piece of writing

TIME OUT, TAKE FIVE
Journal entry: On the receiving end

USING JOURNALS
Task 7: Very truly yours
Using dialogue journals in the classroom

HOMEWORK
Task 8: Tackling it yourself
Responding to a piece of learner writing

FURTHER READING
References about responding to writing

Reflection

TASK 1 'Responding' means...

In this task you think about and discuss different ways that teachers can respond to learners' writing.

Step 1

Work individually.

Read the following twenty statements and decide how far you agree or disagree with each one. Circle the letter you choose, as follows:

A Fully agree   **C** Mostly disagree
B Mostly agree   **D** Fully disagree

RESPONDING TO WRITING means...

1 praising learners' writing for its strengths.	1	A B C D
2 using a red pen.	2	A B C D
3 correcting every single error.	3	A B C D
4 providing correct answers for learners.	4	A B C D
5 learners rewriting answers after teachers have corrected them.	5	A B C D
6 giving specific feedback to learners (e.g. remarks about past tense questions).	6	A B C D
7 correcting some errors, leaving others alone.	7	A B C D
8 getting learners to cooperate (e.g. give feedback to each other).	8	A B C D
9 giving marks for grammatical accuracy.	9	A B C D
10 reacting to *what* learner writers express (the content).	10	A B C D

11 reacting to *how* learner writers express something (e.g. the form, the organisation).   11 **A B C D**
12 sometimes using a green, purple or pink pen.   12 **A B C D**
13 encouraging learners to experiment with new language (e.g. vocabulary).   13 **A B C D**
14 collecting important errors for analysis by the whole class.   14 **A B C D**
15 insisting on correct grammar.   15 **A B C D**
16 helping learners self-correct.   16 **A B C D**
17 using correction symbols to indicate errors (e.g. S = spelling error, P = punctuation error).   17 **A B C D**
18 encouraging learners to write enthusiastically.   18 **A B C D**
19 asking learners to evaluate their own writing.   19 **A B C D**
20 giving a general mark for content and form.   20 **A B C D**

Step 2

Work in groups.

Imagine you are learners. How would you like your teacher to respond to your writing? Discuss which type of teacher response to writing you think is *ideal*. Include in your ideal response at least four items from Step 1. Be ready to share your ideas with the rest of your class.

TASK 2 Taking the plunge

In this task you respond to a piece written by a learner as if you are his teacher. You then reflect on the reasons for your response.

Step 1   **I**

1 Read the profile of the learner, Henny, and his writing task.

Profile of the learner: Henny

- 13-year-old boy
- 3rd year of English study
- Class has five 50-minute English lessons a week
- Class recently reviewed past tense and present perfect tense
- Henny has not yet studied the passive voice (e.g. *was taken*, *had been found*)

Henny's writing task

Write your own conclusion to the story we read in class. Use your imagination!

---

2 Your trainer will provide a copy of Henny's story for you. Read it through.

3 Imagine you are Henny's teacher. Think about the type of response you are going to write to him. Before you write your response, think about these questions:

a What colour ink will you use?
b How will you indicate or comment about Henny's grammar?
c Will you comment on the organisation of his ideas?
d Will you comment about the content of his work?
e Will you use correction symbols (e.g. S = spelling error)? If so, which ones?
f Will you indicate the errors (e.g. by underlining or circling them) or will you write in the correct form of the errors?
g Where will you respond or write comments (e.g. in the margins, in the body of the text or in a separate paragraph at the end)?
h Will you give an overall mark to Henny? If so, how will you decide on your mark?

4 Imagine you are Henny's teacher and write your response on his work, as if it is in his exercise book.

Step 2

Work in groups.

1 Read and discuss your responses to Henny's writing. What do you like or dislike about each other's responses?

2 Discuss the Focus questions on page 85.

Focus questions

1 *a* What kind of response from you as a teacher would help to develop Henny's *fluency* in writing?

b What kind of response would help Henny to write with more *accuracy*?

2 *a* If you had to, what overall mark would you give to Henny for his writing?

b Give reasons for your chosen mark.

c What are two advantages of giving Henny an overall mark?

d What are two disadvantages of giving him an overall mark?

Responding

TASK 3 If u kn rd ths...

In this task you use symbols as a means to give feedback, then reflect on the value of using such symbols.

Step 1 **I**

Work individually.

1 *either*

a Make a list of any symbols that your teachers have used when responding to your writing. What was the meaning of each symbol (e.g. S = spelling error)?

or

b If your teachers did not use symbols when responding to your writing, what symbols might they have used? Invent five (e.g. S = spelling error).

2 Add to your list some symbols which you could use to give positive feedback. Include the meaning of your symbols (e.g. = that's great).

Step 2 **P**

Work in pairs.

1 In the left-hand column of the table **Correction symbols** (p. 86) are some symbols that a teacher might use when responding to learners' writing. In the middle column is an explanation of each symbol. Add any extra symbols from Step 1 which you would like to use as a teacher, together with your explanations.

2 Look at Henny's assignment again. In the right-hand column of the table, **Correction symbols**, write down *one* example of each type of error in Henny's text. An example has been done for you.

Step 3 **P**

Work in pairs.

1 Imagine you are Henny's teachers. You are going to use symbols to respond to his work. Before doing that, discuss the following:

a Which errors will you indicate (e.g. all his errors, or only those which interfere with understanding)?

b How will you indicate where Henny's errors are (e.g. circle them, underline them with a wavy line)?

c Will you use symbols to give positive feedback to Henny? If so, which ones?

d Which symbols (from Step 2) will you use?

e Where will you put your chosen symbols (e.g. in the margins, above each error)?

2 Based on your discussion, write your chosen symbols together on Henny's paper, as if you were his teacher. Write directly on the page, as if you are going to hand it back to Henny.

Step 4 **G**

Work in groups and discuss the Focus questions.

Focus questions

1 Exchange papers and look at each other's responses. How were your responses different?

2 Explain to each other your reasons for responding in the way you did.

3 *a* Which is the most important type of error to focus on in Henny's work?
b Why?

4 How important is it to give positive feedback?

5 If you did **Task 2 Taking the plunge** (p. 84), how have your ideas about responding to a piece of learner writing changed since then?

CORRECTION SYMBOLS		
SYMBOL	**EXPLANATION**	**EXAMPLE**
S	spelling error	
P	punctuation error	
V	verb tense error	
WO	incorrect word order	
WW	wrong word used	
Agr	agreement (subject-verb, adjective-noun or noun-pronoun)	
//	new paragraph needed	
R-O	run-on sentence	*line 1: ...in her Haus probably she...*
^	something's missing	
☺	good; well done; I like this	
?	I don't understand this	
(Add more here)		

TASK 4 A bird's eye view

In this task you learn how to respond to the organisation and content of a piece of writing.

Step 1   **I**

Work individually.

Read the Profile of the learner: Margareta, and her writing task.

Step 2   **P**

Work in pairs.

Read Margareta's letter to Jagdeesh provided by your trainer, then discuss the Focus questions about the organisation and contents of her letter. *Ignore Margareta's grammar, spelling and punctuation errors.*

Profile of the learner: Margareta

- 16-year-old girl
- 4th year of English study
- High intermediate level
- Class has English lessons three times a week for 45 minutes

Margareta's writing task

In the previous lesson the learners read and discussed an ad from *Fortune* business magazine, in which one caption read *You needn't be ashamed of wanting to be something in life.* The class had a discussion and some learners did not agree that success means having a lot of money. The teacher asked the learners to write a letter to their Indian penfriend, Jagdeesh, who asked them in his last letter what it meant to them to be successful in life.

Focus questions

1 What are the main ideas of Margareta's letter?

2 How many different ideas are there in each paragraph?

3 *a* Find one of Margareta's main ideas that is supported by insufficient detail.
b What extra information might Margareta add to support the main idea you found in (a)?

Step 3   **I**

Work individually.

Respond to Margareta, as if you were her teacher. Limit yourself to three sentences or three minutes, whichever is shorter, as you have 30 other learners' assignments to review. Comment *only* on the overall organisation of her ideas and the contents and suggest practical ways to improve her letter. Ignore all grammar, spelling and punctuation errors.

Step 4   **G** and **C**

Work in groups.

1 Read all of the responses to Margareta's letter in your group.

2 Decide which response best addresses the organisation and contents of Margareta's writing and how it does this.

3 Read out your best response to your class and give your group's reasons for your choice.

TASK 5 Tips from teachers

In this task you read about and reflect on how some teachers treat errors in learners' writing.

Work in groups.

Answer the Focus questions as you read the teachers' opinions below and on page 88 about responding to writing, then discuss your answers with your group.

Focus questions

1 Which good new ideas did you read about responding to writing?

2 *a* Which teacher's ideas might you follow if you were working with beginners? Why?
b Which ideas might you use with advanced classes? Why?

3 Which ideas would you avoid if you were working with large classes (e.g. classes of 30 or more learners)? Why?

4 Which tips would you use for teaching children or teenagers and which for adults? Why?

TEACHERS' OPINIONS ABOUT RESPONDING TO WRITING

I believe that errors aren't necessarily bad habits that my learners have picked up. Sometimes they are very creative indications of their trying out new forms, based on their own ideas about how the language works. They're hypothesising and sometimes they get things right.

Amanda

I like to give my learners marks for their writing. I usually use a 30 point scale and I divide that up further: I give up to 15 points for content, 10 points for organisation, and 5 points for grammar. I want them to become more fluent writers who feel confident and motivated to take risks, so I deliberately keep the emphasis on what they're saying, not so much on how they're saying it.

Kala

I find that my learners, all in their early teens, really like a little friendly competition in the classroom. So I do things like give out prizes such as posters and comic books to encourage them to write well – they get so many points for each piece of writing, and the points can be added up for prizes. My friend who teaches businessmen says that my system wouldn't work for her learners. They are serious about learning and expect learning to be serious! To motivate them, she says she brings in samples of their own writing and shares them with the whole class, who look them over for errors and try to correct them. Apparently, this really motivates her group, but I think that it would make my learners too self-conscious.

Johan

I do believe that learners expect a teacher to correct their writing, so it undermines them if I don't make any remarks on their errors. But they understand that first they are to look for their own mistakes and see if they can correct them. Sometimes we do this in groups, and then I give the class more input if they need it. Also, I often collect a few common mistakes and write them on the board for the whole class to correct.

Eve

I think it's really important to 'talk' to my learners when they write, to respond to what they say more than how they say it. I like to give some kind of personal comment about what they've written and usually mention something about my life, too.

Frank

I like to publish my learners' writing whenever possible. Sometimes we do a newsletter for the school, other times we simply display their writing on our walls. It helps motivate learners to write well and more carefully edit their own work for mistakes. They're really proud when their work is published.

Ishmael

When I sit down to read my learners' papers, I try to avoid holding on to any pen or pencil, especially a red one! I also try to read the entire piece of writing through once and think about the whole thing, before lifting my pen to mark anything.

Guus

I once read that the human mind can only hold seven pieces of information in its memory at any one moment. After that I stopped correcting, or even pointing out, all the errors my learners made in their writing. I figured that they couldn't remember them all even if they wanted to! Now I focus my attention, and theirs, on one or two items only – like a structure we practised in class last week – and I think the feedback helps them.

Bartholomew

Sometimes I use a correction key to indicate the type of errors made and sometimes the learners use the same key when they edit each other's work. It's a nice short-hand way of showing that something's wrong.

Doreen

I help my learners select their best projects to put into a portfolio. This portfolio is then reviewed at the mid-point and end-point of the year to measure the learners' progress, and believe me, even the learners who started out in the bottom third of the class are able to see some progress and feel more confident that they can improve, with effort.

Leni

When I see several errors made by learners of the same L1, I try to figure out what the cause of the errors could be. Perhaps there is something in their native language that is similar and that's why they make that mistake.

Haluk

TASK 6 Bravo!

In this task you evaluate and write comments about the strengths of a piece of learner writing.

Step 1   **I**

Work individually.

Re-read Margareta's letter from **Task 4: A bird's eye view** (your trainer will provide you with a copy). Think now *only* about the good points in her writing. Make notes on:

a good points about the content of her writing
b good points about her organisation
c good points about her grammar.

Step 2   **I**

Work individually.

Imagine you are Margareta's teacher and you have 30 other letters to read. Write a short, encouraging remark to her. In your remark, say what is good about her writing: be specific and brief.

Step 3   **P**

Work in pairs.

Compare your comments with a partner and discuss how Margareta might feel when she receives your comments.

Time out, take five

> ### Journal entry
> ### On the receiving end
>
> Think back to pieces of writing for which you received feedback from your teachers. What kind of positive feedback did you receive? Did the teachers comment on your strengths or not? Did the teachers respond to content and form? How did you feel when you received their feedback? If you had been in their place, how would you have given feedback? Why?

Using journals

TASK 7 Very truly yours

In this task you explore using dialogue journals with your learners.

Step 1   **C**

Work as a whole class.

What do you already know about journal writing with learners of English? Brainstorm your ideas with the rest of the class using the question words below.

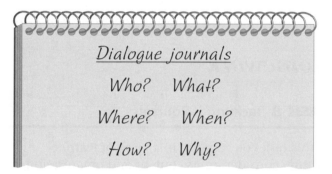

Dialogue journals

Who?   What?

Where?   When?

How?   Why?

Step 2   **P**

Work in pairs.

Your trainer will give you two examples of journal entries written by learners and their teachers. Fill in the missing information surrounding them. You may have to guess.

Step 3   **I**

Work individually.

The following was written by Elizabeth, a 12-year-old whose level is high-intermediate. Respond to this journal entry as if you were Elizabeth's teacher.

> **ELIZABETH'S JOURNAL**
>
> What would you do if someone you knew was running away. They had the money to go to San Francisco or San Diego. They had about $1,000. You had already tried to convince them to stay but they were still going to. Would you tell their parents? What would you do?

Taken from *Dialogue Journal Writing*

Step 4

Work in groups and discuss the following Focus questions.

Focus questions

1　Look at the teachers' responses to Catalina's, Miguel's and Elizabeth's journal entries (including your own response to Elizabeth's journal).

a　Does the teacher correct errors?
b　Does the teacher address the learner's ideas?
c　Does the teacher introduce a new subject? If so, why?

2　Would the teacher give the learners a mark for these journals? Why/why not?

3　What topics might a teacher suggest that her 13-year-old learners write about in a journal if they have been learning English for two years?

4　How can dialogue journals be used in a large class?

5　How can dialogue journals be used with beginners?

6　What are two advantages of using dialogue journals when teaching or learning English?

Homework

TASK 8　Tackling it yourself

In this task you respond to a piece of learner writing, considering its content and organisation, strengths and weaknesses.

Work individually.

Step 1

1　Read the following:

> ### Profile of the learner: Jan
>
> - 11-year-old boy
> - beginner
> - has studied English for nine months
> - has English lessons three times a week
>
> ### Jan's writing task
>
> Design your own island and write about it. Use at least eight words from Chapter 9. Use your imagination!

Step 2

Your trainer will provide you with a copy of Jan's piece of writing. Write on it as if you were Jan's teacher. Your response should deal with:

- content
- organisation
- strengths
- errors and areas for improvement.

Spend no more than 15 minutes on this. In a real-life teaching situation, you would not have much time.

Step 3

Note down briefly some comments on your response to Jan's work. Answer these questions:

1　How did you respond to the content of what Jan wrote and his drawing?

2　How did you give feedback on his errors?

3　How did you respond to the organisation of his work?

4　What comments did you make about his strengths as a writer?

5　How did you encourage Jan to improve his writing?

6　Why did you decide to give the sort of response that you did?

7　How does the way you responded to Jan's work compare with the way you originally responded to Henny's story from **Task 2 Taking the plunge** (p. 84)?

Further reading

Bartram, Mark and Richard Walton. 1991. *Correction*. Hove: LTP Publications.
　　Chapters 6 and 7 provide tasks and comments about responding to written errors.

Edge, Julian. 1989. *Mistakes and Correction*. Harlow: Addison Wesley Longman.
　　Easy-to-read book about practical ways of responding to spoken and written errors.

Hedge, Tricia. 1988. *Writing*. Oxford: Oxford University Press.
　　'Chapter 4, Improving', deals with activities such as marking, redrafting and editing.

Makino, Taka-Yoshi. 1993. 'Learner self-correction in EFL written compositions' in *ELT Journal*, 47 (4) October. pp. 337-341.
　　Discusses study showing that guided learner self-correction can, in some cases, be more helpful than teacher correction of written errors.

Peyton, Joy Kreeft and Leslee Reed. 1990. *Dialogue Journal Writing with Nonnative English Speakers: A Handbook for Teachers*. Alexandria, VA: TESOL.
　　A useful guide for teachers who have not had much experience with journal writing.

Peyton, Joy Kreeft, ed. 1990. *Learners and Teachers Writing Together: Perspectives on Journal Writing*. Alexandria, VA: TESOL.
　　Relates the use of journals to a wide range of classroom situations (e.g. deaf learners' writing, interactive teaching of reading).

Raimes, Ann. 1983. *Techniques in Teaching Writing*. Oxford: Oxford University Press, pp. 22, 150-153.
　　These pages suggest practical ways to respond to learners' writing, including content and form, strengths and weaknesses.

12 WE ALL MAKE MISTAKES

Dealing with spoken errors

Reflection

TASK 1 Look where you're going!

In this task, you reflect on your feelings and beliefs about mistakes.

Step 1   ■

Work individually.

Complete these sentences about yourself learning a foreign language:

1 When my classmates made mistakes when they spoke, I felt...

2 When my classmates corrected my mistakes, I felt...

3 When the teacher corrected my spoken language, I felt...

4 The way I like a teacher to correct me is for her to...

Step 2   G

Work in groups.

Discuss your sentences in your group. Choose a group secretary to write down any particularly interesting or problematic areas on the topic of spoken errors that you would like to share with the whole class.

Step 3   ■

Work individually.

The following passage **Reading: Learning steps** deals with the importance of errors in language teaching. Read it and decide how far you agree with the point-of-view of the writer.

Reading: Learning steps

One theory of language learning states that hypothesis testing is a part of our learners' development, and thus learners making mistakes should be viewed as positive (Chaudron 1988:134): language mistakes are a sign that our learners are learning something. It is thus possible to see language errors as 'learning steps' that we can learn from (Edge 1989: 13-17). For example, a student who makes the mistake *I goed** to the cinema yesterday* instead of saying *I went to the cinema yesterday* is aware that a simple past tense is formed by adding *-ed* to the stem of the verb: she does not say *I go** to the cinema yesterday* because her intention is to speak about yesterday. However, she is unaware that the verb *to go* is irregular in the past simple, or she has simply forgotten. She is moving towards correctness in the past tense, although she hasn't quite yet reached her goal. Edge's view is that 'many of the things we call mistakes and see as problems are in fact signals that our students are successfully learning the language' (Edge 1989: 14); our learners are trying things out, testing out their knowledge and skills in learning the language, and making mistakes is a part of their language-learning development. He points out that we should not, therefore, see mistakes as negative. Helping learners by correcting them can be 'a way of giving information, or feedback, to your students, just when it will support their learning' (Edge 1989: 17).

What are errors and mistakes?

TASK 2 Was it an error or a mistake?

In this task, you learn about the difference between an error and a mistake.

Step 1   ▮

Some linguists differentiate between an error and a mistake. Read the following dictionary definition and the reading **Errors and mistakes**.

Dictionary definition

error /ˈerə/ n
(1) (in the speech or writing of a second or foreign language learner), the use of a linguistic item (eg a word, a grammatical item, a SPEECH ACT, etc) in a way which a fluent or native speaker of the language regards as showing faulty or incomplete learning.
A distinction is sometimes made between an error, which results from incomplete knowledge, and a **mistake** made by a learner when writing or speaking and which is caused by lack of attention, fatigue, carelessness, or some other aspect of PERFORMANCE. Errors are sometimes classified according to vocabulary (**lexical error**), pronunciation (**phonological error**), grammar (**syntactic error**), misunderstanding of a speaker's intention or meaning (**interpretive error**), production of the wrong communicative effect, eg through the faulty use of a speech act or one of the RULES OF SPEAKING (**pragmatic error**).
In the study of second and foreign language learning, errors have been studied to discover the processes learners make use of in learning and using a language (see ERROR ANALYSIS).
(2) see under SPEECH ERROR.
see also DEVELOPMENTAL ERROR, GLOBAL ERROR.

Taken from *Longman Dictionary of Applied Linguistics*

Reading: Errors and mistakes

A *mistake*, then, is a slip of the tongue; the learner knows the correct form but has temporarily forgotten it. A learner can probably correct his or her own mistakes. For example, a teacher is asking questions about her learner's weekend. He asks, *What did you do at the weekend, Frits?* Frits answers, *I go**... no, I went to the cinema.* Frits knows that he should answer in the past tense, but forgets for a moment; he then corrects his own mistake. An *error*, on the other hand, occurs because the learner does not know the correct form and so cannot produce it at this stage of learning. Monika, a near-beginner, is talking about what she would like to do in the future, and says, *I like** to be a teacher; I like** to go to Spain next year.* These are errors; because she does not yet know the form *I want to do something*, she uses the present simple tense, which she is familiar with. Errors, however, can show evidence of learning, since learners can be applying rules, either from their own language or from what they know of English, even though at this stage they are getting something wrong.

Step 2   **I** and **G**

Answer the following questions individually, then discuss in groups:

1 Write down some *mistakes* that you often make when you speak a foreign language nowadays. Why do you think you make them?

2 What spoken *errors* have you made recently? Write them down. What caused them?

TASK 3 Don't make a fool of yourself
                            P and **G** and **C**

In this task you reflect on the errors that learners make in English and possible reasons for them.

1 In pairs, make a table as follows. On the left-hand side of the page write three or more English language errors that either (a) you heard recently or (b) are typical of speakers of your language. Include different types of errors: for example,

pronunciation errors, grammar errors or word order errors. On the right-hand side of the page, write down what you consider the cause of each error might be.

Example:

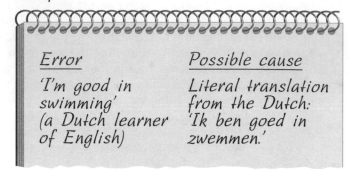

Error	Possible cause
'I'm good in swimming' (a Dutch learner of English)	Literal translation from the Dutch: 'Ik ben goed in zwemmen.'

2 Make a group of four. Share your errors and possible causes and add more to your table.

3 Discuss your answers as a whole class and collect together all the causes of errors that you have thought of.

....

Observation

TASK 4 Whoops!

The aims of this task are to observe and reflect on how a teacher deals with spoken errors.

Step 1   **I**

Work individually.

Use one or more copies of the **Observation table: Spoken errors** provided by your trainer. Arrange to observe an English teacher for one or two lessons. Complete the table as you watch the class; some examples are provided. The lesson will need to involve some speaking, since you are observing spoken errors.

Step 2   **I**

After completing the table, answer the Post-observation questions in writing.

Post-observation questions

As soon as possible after your observation, write down your answers to the following questions. Use specific examples to support your arguments.

1 What kind of errors or mistakes did the teacher correct (for example: a grammatical error, a vocabulary error, a pronunciation mistake)?

2 Why did the teacher correct the errors that you mentioned in question 1?

3 Think about the teacher's error corrections:

   a Would you have acted in the same way or would you have done something else?
   b If so, what might you have done?

4 *a* Were there any errors or mistakes made that you thought should have been corrected but which were not? Give reasons.
   b How might they have been corrected?

5 Were there mistakes or errors made that were corrected but which, in your opinion, should not necessarily have been corrected? Give reasons.

6 Do you have any other comments on error correction in the class you observed?

7 What have you learned from doing this observation task, either related to spoken error or to anything else related to teaching?

Correcting in class

TASK 5 Erroroleplay

In this task you experience different types of error correction and reflect on different ways of correcting errors.

Step 1   G and M

In this task, four different teachers, role-played by you or your classmates, teach four different speaking activities which aim to improve learners' fluency. After each activity write down your answers to the questions below and a few comments about the teacher and particularly about their error correction techniques.

1 What did the teacher do during the task?

2 What did she do after the task?

3 What was her attitude to your errors?

4 Did the teacher correct all the errors made?

5 How exactly did the teacher correct errors?

Step 2   G

Work in groups.

Complete the sentence stems below together. Be as practical and specific as you can.

1 *Teachers should interrupt learners when they make a mistake or error when ...*

2 *Teachers can give delayed feedback in the following situation: ...*

3 *Some errors or mistakes should remain uncorrected by the teacher, for example ...*

4 *Teachers can correct learners in different ways according to the type of tasks which they do, for example ...*

5 *Teachers can vary their error correction strategies according to learners' personalities, by ...*

6 *Teachers can help learners to self-correct or to correct each other's spoken errors by ...*

7 *Some advantages of self-correction and peer correction are ...*

8 *Some disadvantages of self-correction and peer correction are ...*

9 *Five practical ways of giving feedback on spoken errors are ...*

10 *I have learnt the following about giving feedback on spoken errors in this task: ...*

TASK 6 What I would do   **P**

In this task you decide how you would correct some mistakes and errors which occur in a lesson.

Work in pairs.

Discuss each situation and decide:

1 Would you correct the error or mistake?

2 How exactly would you correct it?

3 When exactly would you correct it?

SITUATION 1

You are doing a grammar drill to practise the present perfect tense. You ask, *Have you ever been to the beach?* A student responds, *I've went** to the beach on** France last year.*

SITUATION 2

Your learners are writing a postcard in pairs about their summer holiday to a friend at home. One pair has written, *I am go** to the beach every day.*

SITUATION 3

Your class has just been introduced to the function *Let's do something.* You are organising a trip with your class and you are discussing what to do; a learner says, *Let** go swimming.*

SITUATION 4

You are doing a warming-up activity with your class, asking them about their grandparents. One student tells the class, *My grandmother is three and seventy.***

SITUATION 5

You have just introduced *his* and *hers* for the first time. You have collected some items belonging to your class on your desk. You ask, picking up some keys, *Whose keys are these?* A student answers, pointing at the owner of the keys, *They're him**.*

SITUATION 6

Your learners are working in groups; their task is to plan what to do together at the weekend. Several learners in different groups are making the same mistake, saying, *We go** to a restaurant* or *We go** on a trip.*

SITUATION 7

You are revising tag questions before your class has a test. You are providing sentences; the students must provide the tag questions. You say, *He went to the station...* and point to a student, who says, *Isn't it?*

SITUATION 8

Your class is reading a dialogue aloud from the book in pairs. As you walk around the class and listen to them, you hear that a lot of them cannot pronounce the words *ready* and *happened* correctly.

SITUATION 9

Your class is working in groups, creating a typical day at their ideal school. A learner says, *I liking** Maths and English best.*

SITUATION 10

Your class is working in pairs doing a speaking activity. One student is asking the other to go out for the evening. A student says, *I want** go to a Chinese restaurant.*

Time out, take five

Journal entry
My beliefs about errors

How have my beliefs about mistakes and errors changed after doing this unit?

What have the activities in the unit taught me about other aspects of teaching (e.g. classroom management, giving instructions, setting up activities)?

Further reading

Bartram, Mark and Richard Walton. 1991. *Correction: A Positive Approach to Language Mistakes*. Hove: LTP Publications.
    Practical tasks dealing with spoken and written errors and how teachers can react to them.

Chaudron, Craig. 1988. *Second Language Classrooms*. 'Chapter 5: Teacher and student interaction in second language classrooms.' Cambridge: Cambridge University Press.
    Overview of recent research on errors and feedback.

Edge, Julian. 1989. *Mistakes and Correction*. Harlow: Addison Wesley Longman.
    Easy-to-read book which views mistakes as an important part of learning; practical advice for teachers on when and how to correct mistakes.

Gower, Roger, Phillips, Diane and Walters, Steve. 1995 (New edition). *Teaching Practice Handbook*. Oxford: Heinemann. pp. 164–170.
    Practical advice on error correction.

13 PLAN OF ATTACK

Lesson planning

MAP OF UNIT

Lesson plans

Reflection

TASK 1 Bits and pieces

In this task, you reflect on which elements you
think a lesson plan should contain.

Step 1   ▌

Read this account of an aerobics exercise class.

My example is an aerobics class. I go every Saturday
morning. The teacher had a plan in her head, I think,
and a few notes on paper beside her cassette recorder
to remind her of the exercise sequence, which she
referred to when she changed the cassettes. The aims
of her lesson are always to build up stamina and to
strengthen muscles and her plan is always a sequence
of activities which link together smoothly, moving from
exercising one part of the body to another. The content
of the lesson was exercises for different parts of the
body and we had worked on all parts of the body by the
end of the lesson. It lasted about 55 minutes: the first
20 minutes was stamina work to raise our heartbeats,
then we did 30 minutes' muscle work, and then we
had about five minutes for stretching and relaxation.
At the beginning of the lesson, she welcomed us,
asked if anyone was new, and started exercising after a
few moments, giving us some encouraging comments.
At the end she said we had worked hard and she would
see us next week; she noted who had been present.

Step 2 **P**

Tell each other about a lesson you had, in any subject. This can be any lesson you have experienced as a learner: a sports lesson, a music lesson, a language lesson, etc. Describe the lesson plan that you imagine was prepared for your lesson, using the points a–h on the right.

a the beginning of the lesson

b the aims of the lesson

d what the plan looked like on the page (or in the teacher's mind)

c how the lesson was sequenced

e the balance of activities within the lesson

f transitions (how the teacher linked different stages together)

g the timing of the lesson stages

h the end of the lesson

Step 3 **G**

Work in groups and discuss which of the **Elements of lesson plans** below you would use in a lesson plan for teaching English. Tick those which you would like in your own lesson plan.

Elements of lesson plans

- ❑ number of learners
- ❑ overall aims
- ❑ aims of each stage
- ❑ coursebook used
- ❑ numbers of exercises/activities
- ❑ what the learners do at each stage
- ❑ what the teacher does at each stage
- ❑ materials used
- ❑ homework
- ❑ groupings of learners (individuals / pairs / groups / whole class)

- ❑ aids used
- ❑ timing of each stage
- ❑ skills practised
- ❑ page numbers
- ❑ anticipated problems
- ❑ new vocabulary
- ❑ extra activities
- ❑ age of learners
- ❑ the date
- ❑ interaction (e.g. S↔S or S↔T)

- ❑ different colours for important points
- ❑ review of last lesson
- ❑ sex of learners
- ❑ short description of each activity
- ❑ level of class
- ❑ time of class
- ❑ name/number of class
- ❑ length of class
- ❑ which learners work together
- ❑ abbreviations (e.g. L = learner)

TASK 2 My blueprint **I**

In this task, you evaluate different teachers' opinions about lesson planning.

Work individually.

On this page and page 100 are some teachers' opinions about and strategies for lesson planning. Read them and decide whose opinion you share and which type of lesson plans you would like to make yourself.

I depend on the learners to give me information so I can plan a class. I have a card that goes back and forth every week. I hand out a card to each learner on the beginning of the first day and I ask them to write information on the card: their own name and things like that and also what they think their needs are. And every week I hand back the card and they have an opportunity of adding to the card what they now think they need as opposed to what they did in the beginning. So I have continual feedback from them as I'm preparing.

Sonja

I try to divide my class into approximately 15-20 minute connected micro lessons to create a sense of variety. I use my written plan in class as a check list. I put a check mark next to each item as it is completed. That way I know where I am when I glance at my plan during the lesson, and it is easy to find my place.

Stefanie

I have a general idea of what I want to do in a week but I never plan out the whole week in advance because I never know how far I'm going to get. Basically, I have a notebook which I divide into double pages. Each pair of pages eventually has a whole week of plans on it. The right hand page has the day planned out and it has little notes to myself of what I want to do first, what I want to do second; I even write things down like collect homework, otherwise I forget it. Then the facing page is where I put all my little charts and the examples I want to use. I also write notes there to remind me to talk to learners, because I never remember those type of things but perhaps I want to follow-up on a conversation we had. I always keep my notebooks for a couple of years, and I go back and I refer to them, so I use them a lot.

Cindy

Very often I start writing down things that I want to have in the lesson, in a very chaotic manner, topics and activities, anything: I brainstorm. I start brainstorming, and then usually I have two or three versions and third version is the closest to what it should be like. I simply write down anything that has to be in there and then I re-organise everything. You couldn't really call it a lesson plan.

Krys

I plan everything in my head. All of it. I write a few things down usually. Partly I remember because I've taught courses before, and it's partly improvising as well. Improvising helps me a lot. There are always situations when you plan to do some things, but then you find out that they don't work, so you try something else. The plan doesn't work any more.

Jon

Observation

TASK 3 Deduce the lesson plan

In this observation task you deduce a lesson plan as you observe. *Do not discuss or look at the teacher's lesson plan in advance, but warn the teacher that you would like to see a copy of her lesson plan afterwards!*

Step 1

Observe a lesson, individually or in pairs. As you observe the lesson, write down what you think the teacher's lesson plan looks like, using a copy of the **Observation table: Deduce the lesson plan** provided by your trainer. Alternatively, write the lesson plan in your own personal style on a separate sheet of paper. At the end of the lesson, add what you think were the overall aims of the lesson.

Step 2

After completing the table, answer the Post-observation questions in writing, with your partner if you observed together.

Post-observation questions

1 *a* If possible, obtain a copy of the teacher's lesson plan of the lesson you observed and compare your plan with the original. How does your observed plan differ from the teacher's original plan?
    b Why do the plans differ?

2 Did the teacher do everything that was planned? Why/why not?

3 *a* To what extent were the aims you wrote down the same as the teacher's aims?
    b How might you explain this?

4 What changes would you make in the lesson plan (for example, activities, groupings) if you taught this lesson?

Lesson plans

TASK 4 Topsy-turvy

In this task, you re-order a jumbled lesson and suggest a stage which might follow it.

Step 1   **G**

Work in groups.

Look below at the coursebook extract and the tapescript. The book is the first in a series for beginners in their early teens; the learners have had about thirty English lessons so far. Your trainer will give you a jumbled lesson plan. Re-order it in the way that you would teach it.

Step 2   **G**

Work in groups.

1 Compare your order of the lesson with another group; explain to each other your reasons for your order. (There are several different possibilities.)

2 In your new group, suggest what the next stage of the lesson might be.

Extract from coursebook

Look at the pictures of Joe and Dan King's typical Sundays.
Read the sentences. What does Joe say? What does Dan say? 📼 Listen. Are you correct?

JOE AND DAN KING – A TYPICAL SUNDAY.

a	I have breakfast in bed.	e	I have lunch in bed.	i	I have a shower at six o'clock.	m	I have lunch at one o'clock.
b	I play golf.	f	I don't go to bed on Sundays.	j	I have breakfast at seven o'clock.	n	I play rugby.
c	I go to bed at eight o'clock.	g	I don't study.	k	I write letters.	o	I study Maths.
d	I don't watch television.	h	I don't have a shower on Sundays.	l	I listen to music.	p	I watch television.

Taken from
Fountain Beginners

Tapescript accompanying the coursebook extract

Presenter: Tapescript 48. Listen and check your answers.
  Dan's typical Sunday.
Dan: I have a shower at six o'clock. I have breakfast at seven o'clock. I have lunch at one o'clock. I study Maths. I play rugby. I write letters. I don't watch television. I go to bed at eight o'clock.
Presenter: Joe's typical Sunday.
Joe: I don't have a shower on Sundays. I have breakfast in bed. I have lunch in bed. I don't study. I listen to music. I play golf. I watch television. I don't go to bed on Sundays.

Taken from
*Fountain Beginners
Teacher's Book*

Aims

TASK 5 Aim straight

This task looks in more detail at the aims of the lesson in **Task 4 Topsy-turvy**.

Step 1   **G**

Work in groups.

Opposite are some lesson aims for the lesson in **Task 4 Topsy-turvy**. In the right-hand column, write the letter of the lesson stage which matches an appropriate aim or aims in the left-hand column. One example is done for you. Be careful: there are some extra aims which have nothing to do with this lesson!

Step 2   **P**

Work in pairs.

Read the **Types of aims** and **Examples** below. Match each of the **Lesson aims** in Step 1 with a **Type of aim** below.

LESSON AIMS	STAGE
1 Learners come across the present simple tense for the first time.	
2 Learners prepare for a writing activity.	
3 Learners are introduced to Joe and Dan.	
4 Learners listen to discover the answers.	
5 Learners practise using present simple tense.	
6 Learners practise vocabulary from previous lessons.	*b, e*
7 Learners link real-life activities to the lesson.	

TYPE OF AIMS	EXAMPLES
Topic aims	Learners read about a new topic: dinosaurs. Learners discuss capital punishment.
Grammar aims	Learners practise the present perfect tense by writing a grammar exercise from the book. Learners discuss the difference between direct and indirect speech.
Communication aims	Learners talk to each other about what they do every Saturday. Learners reply to letters written to each other.
Vocabulary aims	Learners match pictures of clothing with words. Learners listen for all the words related to school.
Function aims	Learners learn how to greet people in English in different situations (formal/informal). Learners learn how to complain in a shop.
Skill aims	Learners write a holiday postcard. Learners listen to a song and write words in the gaps on the worksheet.
Pronunciation aims	Learners identify the difference between the sounds [/iː/] and [/ɪ/] (listening). Learners read a passage aloud to each other, concentrating on getting the [/iː/] and [/ɪ/] sound correct.
Group dynamics aims	Learners discuss an outing to the theatre for the class. Learners discuss their learning experience this term.
Reviewing aims	Learners revise the vocabulary from the last unit. Learners revise descriptions of places.
Cultural aims	Learners read about recent political events in an English-speaking country.
Organisational aims	Learners correct last week's homework in the workbook. Learners are given their end of year reports.

Evaluating a plan

TASK 6 Face lift

In this task, you evaluate a lesson plan written by a teacher trainee and rewrite it.

Step 1 **P**

Work in pairs.

Look at these photographs taken from a page in a coursebook. What grammar and vocabulary do you think they are being used to teach?

Taken from *Fountain Elementary*

Below is a lesson plan written by a teacher trainee on teaching practice, Helena, using the 'What's my job?' photographs. Her learners have had about twelve English lessons. Answer the Focus questions to help you to evaluate Helena's plan.

Focus questions

1 Are Helena's aims fulfilled by the end of the lesson?

2 Can you add some aims or clarify Helena's stated aims?

3 What could you add at what Helena calls **2 PRESENTATION**?

4 Would you change the variety or type of activities? If so, how?

5 How are the different parts of the lesson linked to each other?

6 What could you change to make the links between the activities smoother?

7 How could you make it clearer what exactly the learners should do at each stage?

8 How is the writing activity related to the rest of the lesson?

9 How might you improve the writing activity to fit in better with the aims of the lesson?

10 What would you remove or add to the lesson?

Step 2   **P**

Work in pairs.

1 Imagine you are teaching this lesson. Together, write your own lesson plan for it.

2 Copy your new lesson plans and circulate them to other members of your class.

HELENA'S LESSON PLAN

LEARNERS:	20 eleven-year-olds; beginners
AIMS OF THE CLASS:	introducing names of different professions
STRUCTURES:	present tense
SKILLS:	all
MATERIALS:	blackboard, chalk, profession photographs, strips of paper with names of different professions on them

---

STAGES

1 REVIEW (15 mins)

    (a) Learners answer the teacher's questions ('What do you usually do in the morning?' etc.)
    (b) Groups of Ls prepare their own puzzles about everyday activities. They mime and the class has to guess what they are doing (I read a book, I wash up, etc.)

2 PRESENTATION (5 mins)

    T presents names of different professions, repeats them twice, shows pictures from the coursebook, writes the names down on the blackboard.

3 ORAL PRACTICE (20 mins)

    T gives Ls strips of paper with names of different professions. Ls read them and mime them. The class guesses what profession they are miming.

4 WRITING (5 mins)

    Ls write 2-3 sentences about what they want to be in the future.

Game

TASK 7 Lesson planning snakes and ladders

In this **Lesson planning snakes and ladders** game, you practise being flexible and improvising when surprises happen. Your trainer will provide the materials for the game. Play the game in groups.

Materials

- A Snakes and Ladders Board
- One pair of dice per group
- One counter per person
- One set of Improvisation Cards per group, copied, cut out and divided into three piles: Teacher Cards, Learner Cards, Surprise Cards
- One set of RULES

Time out, take five

Journal entry:
Why bother with a plan at all?

How important is having a concrete, written lesson plan for you?

Write about the three most vital elements for you in a lesson plan. Explain why these particular parts of a plan are so important.

Further reading

Gower, Roger, Phillips, Diane and Steve Walters. 1995 (New edition). *A Teaching Practice Handbook.* Oxford: Heinemann. pp. 175-187.
   Advice and activities on lesson planning.

Harmer, Jeremy. 1991 (New edition). *The Practice of English Language Teaching*. Harlow: Addison Wesley Longman.
   'Chapter 12: Planning' covers lesson planning, including a detailed example.

Parker, Sue. 'A question of planning.' *Practical English Teaching*. September 1990. p. 25.
   A brief article on thinking about planning your first lesson.

Philpott, Patrick. 'The lesson planner's balancing act.' *Practical English Teaching*. June 1991. pp. 21-22.
   Article about the many factors teachers must juggle to produce a lesson plan.

14 DON'T PANIC!
Classroom management

MAP OF UNIT

REFLECTION
Task 1: Speak for yourself
Discussion about the use of L1 and English in your lessons

▼

OBSERVATION
Task 2: On the move
Observing a teacher's use of body language and teaching space

▼

MANAGING
Task 3: Silent movie
A game to practise body language

▼

MICROTEACHING
Task 4: In the hot seat
Practising your own classroom management skills

▼

TIME OUT, TAKE FIVE
Journal entry: Challenges in classroom management

▼

FURTHER READING
References about classroom management

Reflection

TASK 1 Speak for yourself

In this task, you reflect on using your first language and English when teaching.

Step 1   **P** and **I**

1 Work in pairs.

Together, describe briefly in writing a typical classroom situation in your country (e.g. forty secondary school children aged fourteen, a small group of seven adult learners, a one-to-one lesson).

2· Work individually.

Keeping your classroom situation in mind, look at the statements in the table **L1 or English?** (p. 107) and give each an appropriate score according to your opinion, as follows:

4 totally agree
3 partly agree
2 partly disagree
1 totally disagree

3 Discuss your answers with a partner.

Step 2

There are many good reasons for using mostly English in your classroom with your learners (and outside!). How can you encourage your learners to speak as much English as possible?

Work in groups. Discuss the two Focus questions.

Focus questions

1 Which variables influence how much English you speak in a class?

Example:

> *size of class*
> *learner motivation*

2 What can you do both to encourage your learners to begin to speak English and to keep speaking English? Think of at least *ten* ways.

Example:

> *Speak English yourself as much as possible.*
> *Praise learners when they speak English.*

L1 or English?	
STATEMENT	SCORE
1 A teacher should translate all new vocabulary into L1.	
2 It is best to use English to teach grammar.	
3 A teacher should give instructions first in English and then in L1.	
4 It is not necessary for a teacher to insist on learners speaking English to each other or to the teacher.	
5 A teacher should only use L1 when it is obvious that there is absolutely no other way for learners to understand her.	
6 It's more effective to use English to discipline learners (for example, when asking a class to be quiet).	
7 A teacher needs to use L1 to be able to maintain a good relationship with a class.	
8 It's acceptable to speak L1 to learners outside class.	
9 It's not possible, even with the use of gesture, body language, facial expressions, examples, etc., to communicate clearly in English with beginners.	
10 A teacher should always speak to learners in English in class.	

Observation

TASK 2 On the move

In this observation task, you look at three aspects of a teacher's use of her body: (1) teaching space, (2) eye contact and (3) body language.

Step 1

Work individually.

Draw two large sketches of the classroom you are observing, one for the first part of this task and another for the second part.

Observe a complete lesson, dividing your observation into three parts, as follows:

1 For the first ten minutes, observe the teacher's teaching space.

2 For the second ten minutes, observe the teacher's eye contact.

3 For the rest of the lesson, observe the teacher's body language.

Instructions for each part of the observation task can be found below.

1 Teaching space

Teachers have their own *teaching space* in a classroom; this is the area where teachers mostly prefer to sit or stand in a classroom, the area where they usually feel safe. For the first ten minutes of this task, concentrate on the teacher's teaching space. Each time the teacher moves, draw a line to show where she moves to. Don't worry if your observation sheet looks a bit of a mess! In the box on page 108 is an example of what your observation sheet might look like after a few minutes, with a teacher who moves around a lot. Stop observing teaching space after ten minutes and move on to the next part of your task: *eye contact*.

Example: teaching space

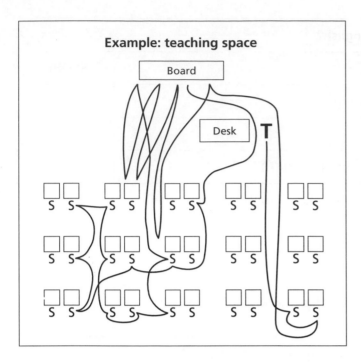

2 Eye contact

For the next ten minutes of the lesson, use your second sketch to note the teacher's *eye contact*. Draw in lines to indicate where the teacher directs her eyes, which learners she makes eye contact with, etc. Again, don't worry if your observation sheet looks a bit of a mess. In the box below is a partly-completed example observation sheet for eye contact for a few minutes of a lesson. Stop observing eye contact after ten minutes and move on to the next part of your task: *body language*.

Example: eye contact

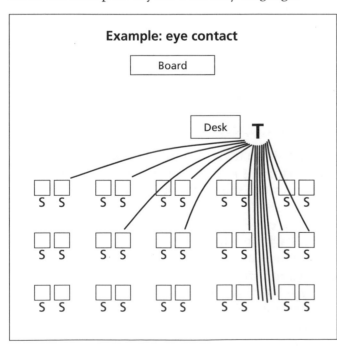

3 Body language

For the remaining part of the lesson, observe what body language (e.g. facial expressions, gestures) the teacher uses to communicate with her class. Try to describe what the body language means in writing. For example:

Body language	Meaning
T uses hands to divide class up	*dividing class*
T raises eyebrows	*surprised by answer*

Step 2   ▮

Work individually.

Answer the Post-observation questions in writing after your observation.

Post-observation questions

1 Teaching space

1 *a* Draw a small square or rectangle to represent the classroom you observed and shade in the teaching space that your teacher used. For example:

   *or*

b Describe the teaching space of the teacher you observed (e.g. *She mostly sat behind her desk.*).
c Suggest reasons why you believe the teacher used that particular space (e.g. *She seemed a bit nervous and 'stuck' to the front of the class and her desk.*).

2 *a* How could the teacher you observed change her teaching space? (e.g. *She could sit less behind her desk.*)
b What might the results be of her moving into different spaces in the classroom?
(e.g. *That would make her classroom manner seem more informal.*)

2 Eye contact

1 *a* Describe the eye contact of the teacher you observed. Which area(s) of the classroom and which learners did the teacher focus on? Give possible reasons for this (e.g. *She only looked at the boys. She seemed to think they needed more attention.*).

b Which areas of the room and which learners did she not make eye contact with? Give possible reasons for this (e.g. *She did not look at the very front rows; she didn't seem to notice learners sitting there.*).

c What were the overall effects of the teacher's use of eye contact? (e.g. *Her eye contact probably made some learners feel more accepted and others ignored.*)

3 Body language

1 *a* Which types of body language did the teacher who you observed mostly use? (e.g. *She used her arms a lot.*)

b How helpful or confusing was her body language in conveying her meaning? (e.g. *Her arm gestures were sometimes confusing and learners didn't understand what she meant.*)

2 Give at least three reasons for using clear body language during a lesson.

Managing

TASK 3 Silent movie   **G**

In this game, you practise appropriate body language to use in a lesson.

Materials per group

• one set of **Silent movie** cards
• a watch with a second hand

Rules

1 Sit in groups around a table.

2 Your trainer will give you a set of cards. Place these face down on the table. Find a watch with a second hand.

3 The first player takes the card from the top of the pile. Do not show it to the group. Written on the card is an action and the part(s) of the body you are allowed to use: you are only allowed to use the part(s) of the body on the card!

Example:

'listen'
(hand/ear)

4 Use body language so that the rest of the group guesses the meaning of what is on the card; for this card, you could cup your hand around an ear to indicate *listen*. The group should time the player: if they don't guess what is meant within one minute, the card, unseen, goes to the bottom of the pile. If the group guesses correctly, player 1 keeps the card.

5 The next player takes the next card.

6 Repeat until all cards have been used.

7 The winner is the player with the most cards at the end.

Microteaching

TASK 4 In the hot seat   **I** and **C** **M**

In this task, you choose an area of classroom management to microteach. Prepare as homework one of the following activities (a–k) to microteach; your activity should not last more than five minutes. If you are new to microteaching, read **3. Microteaching tasks** and **4. Feedback questions** on pages v–vi of the introduction.

> **a.** Find an activity and teach the very start of the activity.

> **b.** Find two activities in a textbook and create a transition between them.

> **c.** Create a situation where you deal with a latecomer.

> **d.** Tell a story using a lot of gestures and mime.

> **e.** Teach a five-minute activity and ask some observers to watch your eye movements.

> **f.** Divide a class of 25 into groups or pairs in an interesting way.

> **g.** Practise ten gestures and ask the class to guess what you mean.

> **h.** Teach an activity with an unconventional classroom furniture or seating arrangement.

> **i.** Practise socialising with three learners who have arrived early (ask three of your classmates to role-play this situation).

> **j.** Teach a short activity and use all the space in your classroom that you can (including the back).

> **k.** Choose an area of classroom management you want to work on and prepare an activity dealing with that area.

Feedback

Give the microteaching trainee feedback on his or her classroom management in particular. Offer suggestions for improvement, especially in the area focused on.

Time out, take five

> *Journal entry*
> **Challenges in classroom management**
>
> Write down **three** areas of classroom management that you would like to improve for yourself and explain why.

Further reading

Gower, Roger, Phillips, Diane and Steve Walters. 1995 (New edition). *Teaching Practice Handbook*. Oxford: Heinemann.
'Chapter 2: Managing the Class.' Sensible advice for trainees on teaching practice.

Nolasco, Rob and Lois Arthur. 1988. *Large Classes*. Hemel Hempstead: Prentice Hall International.
'Chapter 5: Coping with limited resources'. Gives helpful advice on classroom management of large classes.

Nunan, David. 1991. *Language Teaching Methodology: A Textbook for Teachers*. Englewood Cliffs, NJ: Prentice Hall Inc.
'Chapter 10: Focus on the Teacher: Classroom Management and Teacher-Learner Interaction.' Surveys recent literature on classroom management topics.

Richards, Jack C. and Charles Lockhart. 1994. *Reflective Teaching in Second Language Classrooms*. Cambridge: Cambridge University Press.
Chapters 6 and 7 go into some detail about how a lesson is structured and how people interact during lessons.

15 US AND THEM

Learning styles and classroom interaction

Learning styles

Reflection

TASK 1 Curtain up

In this task, you discover your own perceptual learning style by completing a questionnaire.

Step 1 ∎

Work individually.

1 Read these brief descriptions of learning styles: which do you think is your strongest learning style?

Visual learners

You learn better by visual means, for example by reading and by looking at pictures or films. You remember instructions best if you see them, for example on the board.

Auditory learners

You learn well by hearing things, for example lectures or tapes. You like teachers to give oral instructions and you like making tape recordings of what you are learning and having discussions.

Kinaesthetic learners

You learn best when you have hands-on experience, when you are physically involved or can actively participate. You like moving around when you learn and you also like a variety of classroom activities.

---

2 Now complete the questionnaire about learning styles provided by your trainer and calculate your total scores.

Step 2   **G**

Discuss the following Focus questions in groups.

Focus questions

1 Which is your primary learning style: visual, auditory or kinaesthetic?

2 Do you have one strong and one weak learning style, or do you have an even mixture of styles?

3 Does this agree with what you predicted in Step 1?

4 Which is your weakest learning style: visual, auditory or kinaesthetic?

5 How could you improve your weakest learning style?

6 How might your learning style influence your teaching style?

....

TASK 2 Acting out

In this task, you discuss how you can accommodate your learners' different learning styles in your teaching.

Step 1   **G**

Work in groups. Try to have people with different strong learning styles in each group. Discuss the following:

> You yourself use a mixture of learning styles. In your classes, too, there will be different learners with different learning styles. How can you help them to learn better? Think about each learning style in turn. Write down five more pieces of advice that you, as teachers, would give to each type of learner in order to help them study and learn more efficiently. Some examples are given to start you off.

Visual learners

1 Write things down.

2 To help you stay focused, look at people who talk to you.

3 Look at the pictures and models in a chapter before you read it.

Auditory learners

1 Study out loud with a friend or alone.

2 Ask your teacher for oral instructions if you don't understand.

3 Play tape recordings to yourself about what you are studying, or make them yourself.

Kinaesthetic learners

1 When you are learning, walk around the room or change your position every so often.

2 Take short breaks often, say every 20 minutes or so.

3 Highlight or underline your notes or draw things on them.

Step 2   **P**

Work in pairs.

As a teacher, you can teach in a way that helps each type of learner to understand. For example, if you present the word *hippopotamus* to your class, the visual learners will like it if you show them a picture of a hippo and ask them to write the word down, the auditory learners will appreciate saying the word and hearing it, and the kinaesthetic learners will enjoy an exercise where they have to match pictures with definitions.

1 Imagine you are presenting these new words:

saxophone   Italy   downstairs

Design a presentation which will accommodate the three types of learning styles discussed in this task.

2 Share your ideas with another pair.

Classroom interaction

Reflection

TASK 3 Many hands make light work

In this task, you think about groups you have belonged to and then reflect upon what makes a group successful or not successful.

Step 1   **I**

Work alone.

1 Write down some groups that you have belonged to, or belong to now.

Example:

> GROUPS
> my Spanish class
> committee for newsletter at school
> group of four friends
> (since beginning of school)
> my dance group

2 Choose one group that you really like and write down **two** aspects which make a successful group effective.

Example:

> DANCE GROUP
> - really nice atmosphere
> - everyone contributes
>   and works hard

3 Think about the group which you don't like and write down **two** aspects which make a less successful group less effective.

Example:

> COMMITTEE
> - one person takes all the decisions
> - I don't feel at ease with everyone

Step 2   **G**

Work in groups.

1 Looking at your notes for Step 1, make a list of what you consider makes an effective, or successful group. List at least **five** aspects.

Example:

> Group members are tolerant of one another.

2 Make a similar list of some aspects of an unsuccessful group. Again, list at least **five** aspects.

Example:

> There is a lot of arguing.

3 Share your ideas with the rest of the class.

Step 3   **P**

Work in pairs.

Look back at the groups in your first list in Step 1 and read about the stages of group development on page 114. Identify the stage of development for each of your own groups and explain why you think they are at that stage.

Example:

> I have just joined a group for a tennis lesson. We are getting to know each other, so the group must be at the forming stage.

STAGES OF GROUP DEVELOPMENT

Group dynamics theory recognises that groups have a life of their own, and that every group goes through similar stages of development[1]. These five stages can be simplified and characterised as:

FORMING Group members are getting acquainted, and are rather anxious; they are full of expectations and questions about being in the group.

NORMING The group is beginning to become a recognised group where members accept each other. Norms and values emerge.

STORMING In this stage, group members commonly have conflicts and there is a lack of unity.

PERFORMING The group is working well together and a sense of group identity emerges. Conflicts are coped with effectively. The group has become an entity and can solve problems constructively together.

MOURNING The group is ready to come to an end and if it has worked well then this stage can be painful and upsetting, since individuals must go their own way and say goodbye.

Observation

TASK 4 Criss-cross

In this observation task, you observe interaction patterns in a classroom; in other words, you record who interacts with whom and how often.

Step 1

Work individually.

1 Draw a bird's eye view of the classroom you are going to observe. Draw in the desks, the board, the windows, the door and the teacher's table. Indicate where boys and girls are sitting, with some sort of sign (e.g. B/G); alternatively, write the learners' names in their places. Your plan might look something like this:

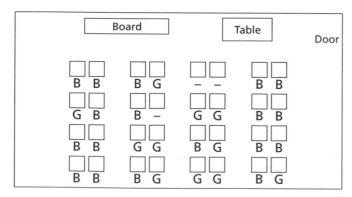

[1] Tuckman 1965, Stanford 1990, Heron 1989. Tuckman places storming before norming.

2 After a few minutes have passed, draw in the interaction patterns that occur in the classroom. Do this for about 10-15 minutes, as follows:

⟶   T says something to a S
⟵   or S says something to T
      or S says something to another S
      (the arrow indicates the direction of the interaction and between which people)

×   T asks a question to the whole class
     (place one × beside the teacher to indicate each question)

Use any other symbols that you find helpful as you record the interaction in the classroom, and say what they mean.

Example:

---?-<---   Question from S to T or vice versa

---!*!*---   Argument between two people

A partially completed interaction pattern might look like this:

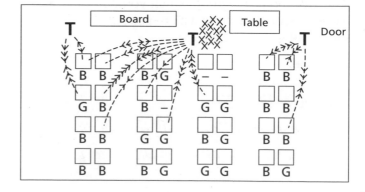

Step 2   I

Work individually.

After completing the observation, answer these Post-observation questions in writing.

Post-observation questions

1 Comment on the interaction patterns of the teacher you observed:

a Describe the areas where the teacher concentrated her attention. Did she interact with one area of the classroom, or one row, or one type of pupil, or one pupil, or with all of the class? Why?

b Does the teacher have a 'blind spot' in her classroom, i.e. a place where she never looks? Why?

2 In your opinion, what should you pay attention to when you are interacting with a class? Why?

Interaction

TASK 5 It takes all sorts

In this task you read one teacher's problems with mixed ability classes, then evaluate and suggest advice for handling similar problems.

Step 1   P

Work in pairs.

1 On your own, read Chitra's letter to an English teachers' magazine. As you read, note two major problems she describes.

2 *a* With your partner, list the major problems Chitra faces.

b Which of her problems are common to teaching situations in your teaching context?

c How do you think a teacher can handle each problem from (b)? For solutions, draw upon lessons you have experienced as learners, as trainees or as teachers.

CHITRA'S LETTER

Dear Editor,

Thank you for inviting English teachers from around the world to write to you about our teaching situations. I enjoy reading your magazine every month — there are always so many new and exciting ideas in each issue! Yet I have to admit that I often feel a bit discouraged after reading about many of these communicative ideas. I think they would be really hard to put to work in my situation. Let me explain.

I work in a secondary school which is very crowded — classes are really large — and I am the only qualified English teacher for our whole school. All over my country people want to study English but it is difficult to find good teachers. The Ministry of Education can't pay school teachers very much, so many teachers leave the schools in order to teach privately. That's why we often have only one or two English teachers for the entire school. I teach several sections of classes and have too many learners to respond to. It's very frustrating, especially when you want to do some communicative activities with them.

Besides having very crowded classes, my classes are also quite mixed in ability. In my case, that means having some high-beginners in the same class as some more intermediate-level. Some learners have been sent to private language schools in addition to the regular classes they get in school, so they are usually ahead of the rest of the learners and consequently bored. My school director says we can't move these upper-end learners into a different section; they have to stay with the same class. I feel torn since I know that they will be bored, yet the rest of the class (usually about two-thirds of each class) are not at such a high level.

It seems that whatever I do, I can't please everybody. Some days I just don't know what to do. Isn't there someone who could give me some advice? I would be very grateful for any help you or your readers could offer.

Yours sincerely,

Chitra

Step 2 **I** and **P**

Work individually. Read the advice contributed to the magazine by four other teachers, then discuss with a partner what advice you would offer Chitra.

Dear Chitra,

I also have to teach large classes – it is a lot of work! But I do try to make the lessons communicative, at least some of the time.

I use a lot of pair and small group work, which means that the groups are often unmonitored, but at least they get a chance to talk. You can't learn to talk without talking, after all!

– Sarah, Indonesia

Dear Chitra,

I think most of us have classes with mixed abilities, at least at some level.

A tip I've found helpful is to group the students by level, so that the upper-end students are working on a more complex version of the same task that the lower-end students are working on.

For example, in learning about apologising, the lower-level learners are learning phrases for the first time and perhaps filling in one line missing from a dialogue. The upper-level students,

meanwhile, are also working on apologising, but they have to write their own dialogue and perform it for the class. They can be good role models and inspiration for other learners.

– Tomek, Ukraine

Dear Chitra,

I think one of the biggest challenges in mixed ability classes where there is a fairly wide spread is to refrain from labelling some students as 'slow' or 'dumb' and others as 'quick' or 'bright'.

I find I have to bite my tongue to keep from referring to them in this way, especially when I am talking about them with other teachers.

I find it can be helpful to see how the students who are struggling are doing in other subjects as well, not only English, and discuss their progress with their other teachers. It may be a question of their not having good study habits or positive role models outside of school to help them progress.

– Jinan, China

Dear Chitra,

When I have large classes, I inevitably end up doing some choral repetition and lots of group work, when I'm circulating around to check their work and answer questions.

But in terms of the make-up of the groups, I try to let the students pick their own groups to work with. They usually seek out students who are at a similar level (and often, are their friends). In cases where they want to work with students of a very different level, I try to enforce a 'buddy system' where the upper-end student is given credit for serving as a coach. Not on exams, of course, but in working on oral homework. They like it, but I have to make sure that everyone is comfortable with this arrangement. We usually negotiate it at the beginning of the term.

– Michael, Nigeria

TASK 6 Problem-solving

In this task, you discuss case studies to do with class relationships.

Step 1 **G**

Work in groups.

On this page and page 117 are four real case studies, written by teacher trainees. Read them through and then discuss how you would deal with the people involved in the case studies. Think of as concrete a solution as possible for each case.

CASE STUDY ONE: GRAMMAR

I was trying to explain the difference between the past tense and the present perfect tense, using six pictures in the book. As the pictures were not very clear, the class started to argue with me and ask me difficult questions, trying me out. I got involved too much in the discussion and started to get angry, because I was not prepared for this to happen. I could not control the class anymore, so I simply stopped the exercise and said they could do it for homework.

Mina

CASE STUDY TWO: GEORGI

One of my pupils, Georgi, knows me because he lives in the same street as I do; he knows personal details about me, such as who my boyfriend is and who my brothers are, etc. This in itself is not really a problem for me, but because Georgi knows me personally he refuses to treat me as his teacher. He doesn't call me 'Miss' or anything and he is a bit cheeky. It never gets really bad – he doesn't embarrass me, for example – but I feel uncomfortable having him in my class; I generally just ignore him. I think I'm scared of teaching people I know personally, especially on teaching practice.

Andrea

CASE STUDY THREE: KARA

At the beginning of my teaching practice, I had a conflict with one of my students, Kara. I wanted the students to do a pair work activity, and I decided who worked together so they were not the usual pairs. Kara objected and said she wanted to work with her friend. I responded that I would like her to work with the girl I suggested. She answered that if I continued, she would not cooperate and not do the pair work. I looked at her angrily, and said she should not do that, because I could make life difficult for her, too.

Jon

CASE STUDY FOUR: FREDDY

I gave my class some homework and was checking it the next morning. There I was, standing in front of 30 pupils, feeling rather nervous and hoping that everyone had done their homework. I had decided to ask oral questions to check the homework. Before I even had a chance to ask the first question, a boy called Freddy told me that he had not done the homework. My first reaction was to ask him what his reason was. I then heard him whispering to his neighbour that he didn't want to do that boring stuff.

Roula

Step 2 **G**

Work in groups.

1 Together, choose one of the case studies.

2 Two or more of you role-play your situation and try to solve it, one being the teacher and the other(s) being the individual or class involved; the other group members should be observers and give feedback and suggestions for improvement.

3 When you have done one role-play, choose another case study for other group members to role play.

4 Repeat as often as you like, with different combinations of role-players interacting with each other.

TASK 7 Virtual reality[2]

In this task, you experience three short simulations about relationships related to teaching.

Work in groups of three.

Step 1 **G**

1 Label yourselves A, B and C.

2 Read your own role card (provided by your trainer) for Simulation 1. Role A is an English learner; Role B is an observer; Role C is an English teacher.

3 Do the simulation for ten minutes.

4 Discuss the simulation briefly, the observer giving feedback to the others.

Step 2 **G**

1 Read your own role card (provided by your trainer) for Simulation 2. Role A is an observer; Role B is a teacher training director; Role C is a native-speaker English teacher.

2 Do the simulation for ten minutes.

3 Discuss the simulation briefly, the observer giving feedback to the others.

[2] At a workshop in Jedlińsk, Poland, Carol Breeding inspired us to use simulations in teacher training.

Step 3

1 Read your own role card (provided by your trainer) for Simulation 3. Role A is a teacher trainer; Role B is a teacher trainee; Role C is an observer.

2 Do the simulation for ten minutes.

3 Discuss the simulation briefly, the observer giving feedback to the others.

Step 4

Have a class discussion on the following Focus questions about the simulation.

Focus questions

1 What did you do well in the simulation?

2 What did you do badly in the simulation and how might you have 'performed' better?

3 What kinds of behaviour or words helped the communication in each conflict?

4 What kinds of behaviour or words hindered the communication in each conflict?

5 As an outside observer, what did you notice that you did not tend to see while in role?

6 Discuss anything else you found interesting about the experience of doing this simulation.

....

Microteaching

TASK 8 Actions and reactions

In this task, you teach a group and have to react appropriately to the group's behaviour. If you are new to microteaching, read **3. Microteaching tasks** and **4. Feedback questions** on pages v–vi of the introduction.

Step 1

Work in groups of 8 or 10. One of you will teach an activity and the others will role-play learners.

Teacher Role

At home, prepare to teach the following activity:

> **GUESS WHAT'S IN THE PICTURE**
>
> Find a large, interesting picture with quite a lot of detail in it. The class you are teaching must guess what is in the picture, by asking only yes or no questions. When you think they have guessed enough information, show them the picture.

The other trainees in your group will behave in certain ways according to their role cards. Teach your activity, but keep order by dealing with problems as they come up; don't forget to acknowledge good behaviour as well as dealing with problem behaviour.

Trainees' Roles

Your trainer will give you each a role card; stick to your given role throughout the microteaching, while you participate in the activity.

Step 2

Work in groups to answer the Feedback questions below. (Before your discussion, you might like to show the 'teacher' your role cards.)

Feedback questions

1 How did the teacher deal with the problems that came up?

2 Would you have dealt with any of the problems in a different way? If so, how exactly?

3 Together, prepare some useful comments on the teacher's reactions for the rest of the class.

4 Share your final comments with the whole class.

Time out, take five

Journal entry
Me in a group

Write about yourself in a group that you belong to, perhaps the class you are in now. How do you relate to the class? How does the interaction in the class relate to the class's stage of development and its members' learning styles?

Further reading

Dynes, Robin. 1990. *Creative Games in Groupwork*. Bicester: Winslow Press.
Ideas for games for groups.

Ellis, Gail and Barbara Sinclair. 1989. *Learning to Learn English*. Cambridge: Cambridge University Press.
A practical course to help learners discover their own learning strategies and learn more effectively.

Hadfield, Jill. 1992. *Classroom Dynamics*. Oxford: Oxford University Press.
Practical activities to solve classroom dynamics problems as well as some easily-understood group dynamics theory.

Houston, Gaie. 1984. *The Red Book of Groups*. London: The Rochester Foundation.
Written by a therapist, this slim book contains some easy-to-follow group dynamics theory and some exercises for improving groups.

Hutchings, Sue, Jayne Comins and Judy Offiler. 1991. *The Social Skills Handbook*. Bicester: Winslow Press.
Practical activities for social communication. Ideas for sessions based on group work.

Oxford, Rebecca. 1990. *Language Learning Strategies: What Every Teacher Should Know*. Boston, Mass: Heinle and Heinle.
Practical recommendations for developing learners' second language learning strategies.

Reid, Joy (ed.). 1995. *Learning Styles in the ESL/EFL Classroom*. Boston, Mass: Heinle and Heinle.
Issues in the study of individual learning differences; includes appendix of tests to discover teaching and learning styles.

Richards, Jack and Charles Lockhart. 1994. *Reflective Teaching in Second Language Classrooms*. Cambridge: Cambridge University Press.
Includes chapters on teacher-learner interaction, teacher roles and beliefs, as well as learner belief systems and strategies.

Scarcella, Robin and Rebecca Oxford. 1992. *The Tapestry of Language Learning*. Boston, Mass: Heinle and Heinle.
Examines different learning styles and their impact on our classroom teaching.

Stanford, Gene. 1990. *Developing Effective Classroom Groups*. Bristol: Acora Books.
Theory about classroom groups, plus suggestions for activities for the different stages in a group's development.

Stevick, Earl. 1989. *Success With Foreign Languages*. New York: Prentice Hall International.
Stevick interviews seven successful language learners and explores the language learning strategies they used.

16 YOU CAN'T ALWAYS GET WHAT YOU WANT
Materials evaluation and adaptation

Materials evaluation

TASK 1 Straight from the horse's mouth

In this task you interview two teachers about a
coursebook they use to teach English.

Step 1   **P**

Work in pairs.

1 Find two teachers to interview (ask your trainer
for suggestions).

2 Introduce yourselves to the teachers and explain
why you want to interview them (i.e. to ask their
opinions about a coursebook they use).

3 Together, interview each teacher, completing the
Interview: Coursebook analysis table provided by
your trainer and spending about five to ten minutes
per teacher.

Step 2   **P** and **C**

Work in pairs.

Prepare a summary of the results of your interviews
and discuss them with your fellow trainees.

TASK 2 At first glance

In this task you use a quick assessment test to
analyse a coursebook, called **The MATERIALS Test**.

Step 1   **I**

Read the description of **The MATERIALS Test**. In
Step 2 you will use the test so clarify now any
questions you have about it with your trainer.

Step 2   **P**

Work in pairs.

1 Obtain a coursebook that is used to teach
English. It may be old or new, familiar or
unfamiliar. Use one book for the two of you.

2 *a* Your trainer will provide you with a
Coursebook evaluation chart. Make a quick
note of your initial gut reaction to the book.
b Spend no more than 15 minutes putting the
book to **The MATERIALS Test**, by completing
the chart. Write remarks in the **your comments**
column (e.g. list the actual price under
Affordable, write its level under Level.). If you
don't teach now, try to judge the book in terms
of the type of learners the author states it is
intended for (e.g. 12- to 14-year-olds in a
secondary school, beginners' level).
c Give each aspect of your book a score to make
a final total.

Reading: The MATERIALS Test

A quick assessment of a coursebook can be achieved by evaluating several aspects of the book. Use The MATERIALS Test below to help you. MATERIALS stands for the following:

M	**M**ethod
A	**A**ppearance
T	**T**eacher-friendly
E	**E**xtras
R	**R**ealistic
I	**I**nteresting
A	**A**ffordable
L	**L**evel
S	**S**kills

The MATERIALS Test can help you determine whether a book is worth looking at more closely, outside the shop or away from a publisher's book exhibition. Each of the above aspects can be considered further by asking a few key questions:

 Method

Does the book's method suit your own teaching method and overall aims?

 Appearance

Is the book's appearance – including its cover, design, illustrations, colour and feel – appealing and attractive? Or does it appear dull?

 Teacher-friendly

Is the book easy for the teacher to use? Is it well organised? Is there an index? Does it have an answer key? Does it help you save preparation time?

 Extras

Are there additional materials, such as a workbook, cassette, teacher's notes or separate teacher's book? How helpful are these extra materials?

 Realistic

How authentic is the communication in the book? Does the language seem true-to-life and current?

 Interesting

Is the book likely to be interesting for your learners? How do the topics relate to their lives? Just as important, is it interesting to *you*?

 Affordable

Is the book affordable? Is it worth the price that learners, parents or the school will have to pay?

 Level

Is the level suitable for the class you are teaching?

Skills

Does the book cover all the skills you want to teach (e.g. listening, speaking, reading, writing) in a way you want to teach them? Does it match your institution's syllabus?

3 Discuss your answers to these questions with your partner:

a What strengths did **The MATERIALS Test** reveal in your book?

b What weaknesses did **The MATERIALS Test** reveal in your book?

c How does your **MATERIALS Test** evaluation of the book differ from your initial, gut reactions to it?

d Would you recommend this book for a class of 30 learners who are at the age and level the book says it is intended for? Why/why not? Give *three* reasons for your answer.

Step 3

Work in groups.

1 Imagine you are members of staff of a school. You are meeting to discuss possible coursebooks for your learners.

2 Describe the group of learners that your book is intended for (e.g. level, age, interests).

3 Present your arguments for *or* against the coursebook that you evaluated in Step 2.

Time out, take five

> ### Journal entry
> **Evaluating this book**
>
> By now you have probably had a chance to sample quite a few tasks from this book. What are your impressions of the book? How do you like the tasks? How does doing these tasks with a group help you to be a better teacher?

Materials adaptation

TASK 3 You can't always get what you want

Because each group of learners is different, coursebooks are probably never able to meet *all* the needs of *all* learners and teachers. In this task you think about ways of adapting a coursebook.

Step 1

Work in groups.

Brainstorm all the things that you can think of doing to improve a less-than-ideal coursebook (e.g. bring pictures to class to liven it up). Jot down your ideas.

Step 2   **P**

Work in pairs.

Read the table **You can't always get what you want** below to see whether your brainstormed answers from Step 1 are mentioned, then discuss the following questions with a partner:

1 Which of the four types of action (change, remove, replace, add) have you already had experience with, if any?   .

2 *a* Which requires the most work for the teacher? Why?

b Which requires the least work for the teacher? Why?

You can't always get what you want

Changes of some sort are inevitable if you want a book to fit your aims, your setting, and most of all your learners. There are various actions you can take to tailor a selected coursebook to fit your teaching situation:

Change	**Remove**
Make small changes to the existing material in the coursebook.	Remove a coursebook activity from the lesson.
Replace	**Add**
Replace one activity with another related one which is more suitable.	Add an extra activity in an area not covered sufficiently in the book.

TASK 4 Upon closer inspection

In this task you examine part of a coursebook unit, evaluate some adaptations to some activities in the book and think about how you would adapt it yourself.

Step 1

P and **G**

Work in pairs.

1 Look at the two pages of Unit 1 taken from the coursebook *Mosaic I*.

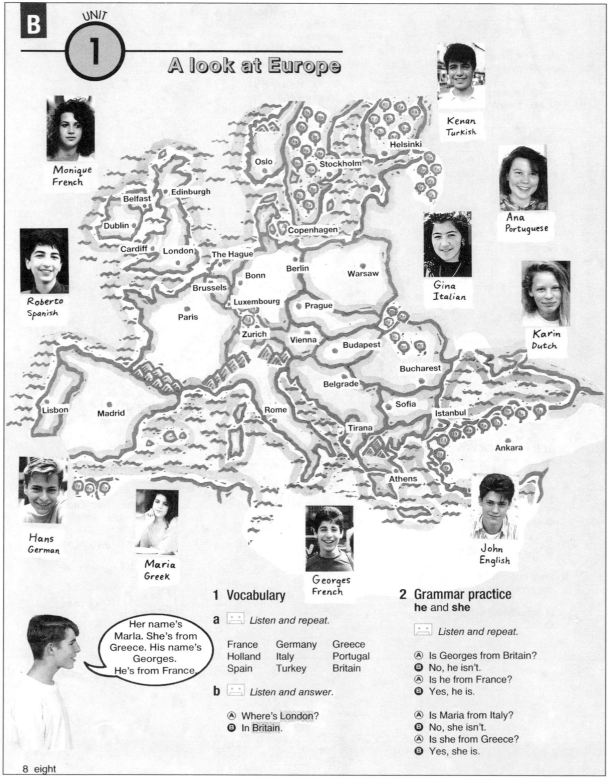

Taken from *Mosaic 1* (reduced)

B

3 Communication

a *Point to a friend.*
Ask and answer with another
friend.

Ⓐ Is _____ from _____?
Ⓑ No, he/she isn't.
Ⓐ Is he/she from _____?
Ⓑ Yes, he/she is.

b *Match the people*
with the countries.

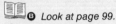
Ⓑ *Look at page 99.*
Ⓐ *Ask. Then answer.*

People	Countries
Maria	Greece
Hans	Germany
Monique	_____
John	
Karin	_____
Roberto	Holland
Gina	Spain
Kenan	Italy
Ana	_____
Georges	France

4 Dictation

😐 *Listen and write.*

Ⓐ W_____'__ Peter _____?
Ⓑ _____'s _____ G_____.
Ⓐ _____ Mary _____ _____?
Ⓑ _____, _____ _____'t.
_____, _____ _____.

5 Grammar practice
his and **her**

a 😐 *Listen and repeat.*

Ⓐ What's his name?
Ⓑ His name's Roberto.

Ⓐ What's her name?
Ⓑ Her name's Maria.

b *Point to a picture or a student.*
Ask and answer.

Ⓐ What's his/her name?
Ⓑ _____.

6 Grammar
I, you, he, she
– my, your, his, her

Write the words.
1 _____ name's Michael.
   _____ from Britain.
            I'm or **My?**
2 _____ name's Gina.
   _____ from Italy.
            Your or **You're?**
3 _____ name's Dimitri.
   _____ from Greece.
            He's or **His?**
4 _____ name's Ana.
   _____ from Spain.
            Her or **She's?**

7 Pronunciation

😐 *Listen, repeat and*
underline.

countries	nationalities
<u>Spa</u>in	<u>Spa</u>nish
<u>France</u>	<u>French</u>
<u>Greece</u>	<u>Greek</u>
<u>Holl</u>and	<u>Dutch</u>
<u>Germ</u>any	<u>Germ</u>an
<u>It</u>aly	<u>It</u>alian
<u>Port</u>ugal	<u>Port</u>uguese
<u>Turk</u>ey	<u>Turk</u>ish
<u>Brit</u>ain	<u>Brit</u>ish

8 Speaking

Talk about the people in the
pictures.

Maria's from Greece. She's
Greek
John's from Britain. He's . . . .

9 Game ◆ *Nationalities*

😐 *Listen. Then play the game.*

10 Study skills
Types of words

Write the words.

I my is France French
he what Greece am you
Spanish Britain British
she Italian her Greek
his are Italy your Spain
where

I	my	what
he		

France	French	am
Greece		

Taken from *Mosaic 1* (reduced)

Imagine you are using this book with the following group of learners:

Class profile

Level: Beginner

Age: 13-14 years old

Class size: 30 (half boys, half girls)

Purpose in studying English: To communicate with tourists/other visitors who speak English.

Other comments: Ls have done some communicative activities in the past and enjoyed them. They seem generally bright and motivated.

---

2 Your trainer will give you a copy of the **Table: Inspecting activities** to complete. In the table, write the activity number(s) corresponding to the categories listed on the left. A few examples have been filled in.

3 Work in groups, by joining another pair to compare your answers. Report your answers to the whole class.

Step 2   **G**

Work in groups.

1 Read the four adaptations of activities in the unit below. Remember the four possible ways of materials adaptation:

Change	Remove
Replace	Add

2 Which of the adaptations to the unit below (change, remove, replace, add) do you like the best? Why? Discuss.

3 Which of the adaptations do you like the least? Why? Discuss.

Sample Adaptations for
***Mosaic I*, Unit 1, activities 1-10**

A Change

Make small changes to the existing material in the coursebook.

Activity to be changed: 5b

> **b** *Point to a picture or a student. Ask and answer.*
>
> Ⓐ What's his/her name?
> Ⓑ _____.

1 *T's aims in changing activity:* To stimulate learner interest in the subject; to encourage fluency through repetition; to introduce humour/laughter to the lesson; to recycle 1st person of verb *to be* (*I'm*) and contrast with 3rd person (*He's…*).

2 *Adaptation:* After activity 5a, each learner assumes the identity of one of the pictured learners, without telling who he or she is. Learners introduce themselves in a chain, using their new identities. LA introduces himself; LB repeats what LA said, then adds her own introduction. Example:

LA: My name's Hans. I'm from Germany.
LB: His name's Hans. He's from Germany. And my name's Monique. I'm from France.
LC: Her name's Monique. She's from France. My name's Kenan. I'm from Turkey.

B Remove

Remove a coursebook activity from the lesson.

Activity to be removed: 10

10 Study skills
Types of words

Write the words.

I my is France French
he what Greece am you
Spanish Britain British
she Italian her Greek
his are Italy your Spain
where

1 *T's aim in removing activity:* To de-emphasise grammatical terminology during first lessons.

2 *Adaptation:* Remove activity 10, study skills.

C Replace

Replace one activity with another related one which is more suitable.

Activity to be replaced: 7

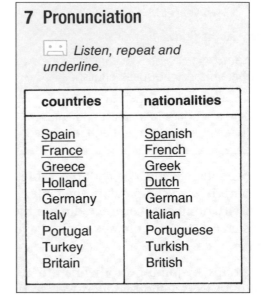

7 Pronunciation

Listen, repeat and underline.

countries	nationalities
Spain	Spanish
France	French
Greece	Greek
Holland	Dutch
Germany	German
Italy	Italian
Portugal	Portuguese
Turkey	Turkish
Britain	British

1 *T's aim in replacing activity:* To increase learner interest, sense of personal relevance to learning English place names.

2 *Adaptation:* Learners draw a map of their own country and label it in English. They add names of several cities and neighbouring countries. They then imagine that they are from different cities in their country and do a role-play introducing themselves.

D Add

Add an extra activity in an area not covered sufficiently in the book.

Activities to be added onto: 4 and 6

1 *T's aims in adding onto activities:* To develop learners' writing abilities.

2 *Adaptation:* Learners bring a photo of themselves to class and create captions for a poster of a group of classmates. They write statements about others in their group, giving them new identities (e.g. 'His name's Marek. He's from Edinburgh.' or 'Her name's Sara. She's from Tel Aviv.'). Posters are put up and read by other members of the class.

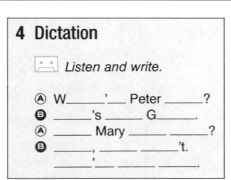

4 Dictation

Listen and write.

Ⓐ W_____'_ Peter _____?
Ⓑ _____'s _____ G_____.
Ⓐ _____ Mary _____ _____?
Ⓑ _____, _____ _____'t.

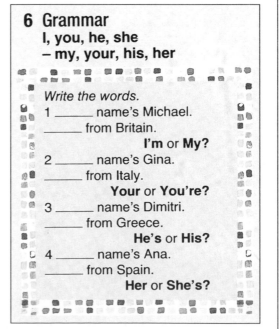

6 Grammar
I, you, he, she
– my, your, his, her

Write the words.

1 _____ name's Michael.
_____ from Britain.
        I'm or **My?**

2 _____ name's Gina.
_____ from Italy.
        Your or **You're?**

3 _____ name's Dimitri.
_____ from Greece.
        He's or **His?**

4 _____ name's Ana.
_____ from Spain.
        Her or **She's?**

Step 3

Work in groups.

1 Choose one activity from **Task 4 Upon closer inspection**, pages 123–6.

2 Decide if you want to change or replace the activity or add a new activity.

3 Brainstorm ideas together for your chosen alteration and then share your ideas with the rest of your class.

TASK 5 Learners do it themselves

This task explores the potential of using materials produced by the learners.

Step 1 **G**

Work in groups.

On a piece of paper, note down in two columns what sort of materials learners can bring to class and how these materials can be used. Here's one example:

> ## Learner-based Materials
>
> | What materials can learners bring to class? | How can learner-based materials be used? |
> | --- | --- |
> | Tape recording of song | Try to understand the words in the chorus |

Step 2 **I** and **G**

Discuss the Pre-reading questions with your group, then read the **Reading: Introduction to learner-based activities** individually to confirm or revise your answers.

Pre-reading questions:

1 What are two advantages of using learner-based activities?

2 What are two disadvantages of using learner-based activities?

> ### Reading: Introduction to learner-based activities
>
> Learner-based activities are those in which the learners themselves provide information or material. One example of a short learner-based activity was already outlined in **Task 4 Upon closer inspection**, on page 126 (**D Add**), as a supplement to a coursebook unit: learners created a poster of their classmates, writing captions for photos. Learner-based activities can be useful in English language classes because they provide opportunities for the learners to make English relevant to their own needs and interests. Also, when learners perform tasks to which they themselves have contributed, they may feel a greater sense of belonging to the class. Thus, such tasks may serve to increase learner motivation, improve class morale, and stimulate learning. Learner-based activities can also be helpful to teachers who have few additional resources available to them (e.g. few native speakers, additional cassettes or workbooks) or who have limited time to prepare supplementary materials.
>
> Regarding the teacher's role, the teacher often serves as a kind of facilitator of the learners' activities, helping to make sure the activity flows smoothly. Depending on the learner-based activity, the teacher may also be an active participant equal to the learners: for example, along with the learners, she may share her opinions while taking care not to dominate the group.

Step 3   **G**

Work in groups. Discuss these questions.

1 **a** Which of the following two learner-based activities would be the most interesting for a group of learners you know (or for one that you can imagine)?

   b Give *three* reasons for your answers.

2 How might you prepare your learners if they have never done learner-based activities[1] before?

3 **a** What are some potential difficulties with your chosen activity?

   b How might you overcome these difficulties?

**Learner-based activity A
Myself as a Star[2]**

Level: Elementary

Time: 20-30 minutes

Language: Simple present, statements and *yes/no* questions, vocabulary describing appearance and personality

Grouping: Whole class

Instructions:

1 Tell the learners they can be anyone in the world. Ask them to imagine what they look like and what their personality is like. Individually, learners draw a large star and in the star they write in eight characteristics of their ideal selves (e.g. athletic, red hair, creative).

2 When individuals have completed their stars, ask one learner to come to the board and draw a big star on it.

3 Tell the other learners they are to guess what the ideal characteristics of the learner are. The class may ask only yes/no questions and the learner at the chalkboard can only answer *Yes*, *No*, or *Sort of*, as appropriate. Whenever a learner guesses a trait correctly, the learner writes that word or phrase in the star. This continues until six characteristics have been identified correctly, or a 5-minute time limit has been reached, whichever comes first.

4 The game continues as the learner at the board chooses another learner to be the star.

**Learner-based activity B
My World and Welcome to It[3]**

Level: Elementary and above

Time: 20 minutes

Language: Names of hobbies, personal interests; simple present, possibly simple past

Grouping: Whole class or in groups of 5-6.

Instructions:

1 Each learner draws a large circle on a piece of paper. Each learner divides the circle up into sections, making a pie chart, according to their own interests and activities. For each interest/ activity, they make a portion of the pie and label it with the activity's name (see sample diagram).

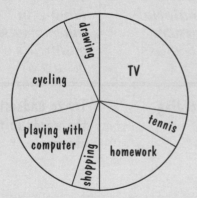

2 Learners attach their charts to their clothes with pins or tape. Learners walk around the room, mingling with others and asking more detailed questions (e.g. *I see you like to watch movies. What kind of films do you like the most?* or *When did you begin to climb mountains? Weren't you scared at first?*).

3 After 10-15 minutes, re-assemble the whole class and ask volunteers to share any especially interesting or surprising information about each other.

---

[1] Many more examples of such tasks can be found in Deller (1991) and Campbell and Kryszewska (1992).
[2] This activity was inspired by 'Character Building' from Campbell and Kryszewska (1992).
[3] This activity was inspired by 'Interest Pies' in Deller (1991).

Further reading

Brandes, Donna and Paul Ginnis. 1986. *A Guide to Learner-Centred Learning.* Oxford: Basil Blackwell.
A book which lays the emphasis on teacher-learner collaboration and activity-based learning.

Brandes, Donna and Paul Ginnis. 1990. *The Learner-Centred School.* Oxford: Basil Blackwell.
Lots on learner-centred learning.

Campbell, Colin and Hanna Kryszewska. 1992. *Learner-Based Teaching.* Oxford: Oxford University Press.
This book contains many ideas for learner-based activities.

Deller, Sheelagh. 1991. *Lessons from the Learner.* Harlow: Addison Wesley Longman.
This book encourages learners to bring their own knowledge and enthusiasm to the classroom by helping them produce their own study material.

Grant, Neville. 1987. *Making the Most of Your Coursebook.* Harlow: Addison Wesley Longman.
This book examines coursebook analysis and selection in a detailed manner. It contains many practical examples of ways to adapt your coursebook or part of it.

Hill, David A. 1990. *Visual Impact.* Harlow: Pilgrims-Addison Wesley Longman.
Lots of ideas for using pictures to practise all English language skills.

Holme, Randal. 1991. *Talking Texts.* Harlow: Pilgrims-Addison Wesley Longman.
A book full of ideas for using written texts.

Murphey, Tim. 1992. *Music and Song.* Oxford: Oxford University Press.
Ideas for using music and songs in the EFL classroom; includes ideas for instrumental music as well as pop songs.

Nunan, David. 1989. *Designing Tasks for the Communicative Classroom.* Cambridge: Cambridge University Press.
This book integrates recent research and practice in language teaching into a framework for analysing learning tasks.

Rinvolucri, Mario and Paul Davis. 1988. *Dictation: New Methods, New Possibilities.* Cambridge: Cambridge University Press.
This book provides numerous examples of learner-generated and learner-led dictations.

Ur, Penny. 1981. *Discussions That Work.* Cambridge: Cambridge University Press.
This book addresses some fundamental issues about analysing and designing tasks for fluency practice.

BIBLIOGRAPHY

Aitken, Rosemary. 1983. *Making Sense (elementary)*. Harlow: Addison Wesley Longman.

Aitken, Rosemary. 1983. *Loud and Clear (early intermediate)*. Harlow: Addison Wesley Longman.

Aitken, Rosemary. 1984. *Overtones (pre-intermediate)*. Harlow: Addison Wesley Longman.

Aitken, Rosemary. 1986. *Play It By Ear (intermediate)*. Harlow: Addison Wesley Longman.

Allwright, Dick. 1988. *Observation in the Language Classroom*. Harlow: Addison Wesley Longman.

Anderson, J.R. *et alia*. 1983. *Integrated Skills Reinforcement: Reading, Writing, Speaking and Listening Across the Curriculum*. New York: Addison Wesley Longman.

Bailey, Kathleen M. 1990. 'The use of diary studies in teacher education programs' in Richards and Nunan 1990.

Bartram, Mark and Richard Walton. 1991. *Correction: A Positive Approach to Language Mistakes*. Hove: LTP Publications.

Beckerman, Howard. 1989. *Guessworks! A Musical Mystery Play*. New York: Collier Macmillan.

Bond, Tim. 1986. *Games for Social and Life Skills*. London: Hutchinson.

Boutin, Marie-Christine, Suzanne Brinand and Francoise Grellet. 1987. *Writing Intermediate*. Oxford: Oxford University Press.

Bowen, Tim and Jonathan Marks. 1994. *Inside Teaching*. Oxford: Heinemann.

Bowers, Roger ed. 1987. *Language Teacher Education: An Integrated Programme for ELT Teacher Training* (ELT Documents: 125). London: Modern English Publications and The British Council.

Brandes, Donna and Paul Ginnis. 1990. *The Learner-Centred School*. Oxford: Basil Blackwell.

Brandes, Donna and Paul Ginnis. 1992. *A Guide to Learner-Centred Learning*. Oxford: Basil Blackwell.

Brinton, Donna, Marguerite Ann Snow and Marjorie Bingham Wesche. 1985. *Content-Based Second Language Instruction*. New York: Newbury House.

Brown, H. Douglas et alia. 1991. *Vistas: An Interactive Course in English*. Englewood Cliffs, NJ: Regents/Prentice Hall.

Campbell, Colin and Hanna Kryszewska. 1992. *Learner-Based Teaching*. Oxford: Oxford University Press.

Carlisi, Karen and Jocelyn Steer. 1991. *The Advanced Grammar Book*. Boston, Mass: Heinle and Heinle.

Carter, Ronald and Michael McCarthy, eds. 1988. *Vocabulary and Language Teaching*. Harlow: Addison Wesley Longman.

Celce-Murcia, Marianne and Diane Larsen-Freeman. 1983. *The Grammar Book: An ESL/EFL Teacher's Course*. Boston, Mass: Heinle and Heinle.

Chaudron, Craig. 1988. *Second Language Classrooms*. Cambridge: Cambridge University Press.

Collins Cobuild English Language Dictionary. 1987. London: Collins.

Cornelius, Edwin T., Jr. 1981. *Interview*. New York: Addison Wesley Longman.

Day, Richard. 1990. 'Teacher Observation in Second Language Teacher Education' in Richards, J. C. and D. Nunan, eds., *Second Language Teacher Education*. Cambridge: Cambridge University Press.

Deller, Sheelagh. 1991. *Lessons from the Learner*. Harlow: Addison Wesley Longman.

Dennison, Bill and Roger Kirk. 1990. *Do, Review, Learn, Apply: A Simple Guide to Experiential Learning*. Oxford: Basil Blackwell.

Doughty, Catherine and Teresa Pica. 1986. '"Information gap" tasks: do they facilitate second language acquisition?' *TESOL Quarterly 20:2*.

Dynes, Robin. 1990. *Creative Games in Groupwork*. Bicester: Winslow Press.

Edge, Julian. 1989. *Mistakes and Correction*. Harlow: Addison Wesley Longman.

Edge, Julian. 1992. *Cooperative Development*. Harlow: Addison Wesley Longman.

Ellis, Gail and Barbara Sinclair. 1989. *Learning to Learn English*. Cambridge: Cambridge University Press.

Ellis, Mark and Printha Ellis. 1983. *Shades of Meaning*. Harlow: Addison Wesley Longman

Ellis, Mark and Printha Ellis. 1984. *At First Sight*. Harlow: Addison Wesley Longman

Enright, D. Scott and Mary Lou McCloskey. 1988. *Integrating English: Developing English Language and Literacy in the Multilingual Classroom*. Reading, Mass: Addison Wesley Longman.

Fanselow, John. 1987. *Breaking Rules: Generating and Exploring Alternatives in Language Teaching*. New York: Addison Wesley Longman.

Frank, Christine and Mario Rinvolucri. 1983. *Grammar in Action*. Oxford: Pergamon.

Freeman, Donald and Steve Cornwell. 1993. *New Ways in Teacher Education*. Alexandria, VA: TESOL.

Gairns, Ruth and Stuart Redman. 1986. *Working with Words*. Cambridge: Cambridge University Press.

Gołebiowska, Aleksandra. 1989. 'Role-plays in Pre-service Teacher Training' in *English Teaching Forum*. Washington, D.C.

Gower, Roger, Diane Phillips and Steve Walters. 1995 (New edition). *Teaching Practice Handbook*. Oxford: Heinemann.

Grant, Neville. 1987. *Making the Most of Your Coursebook*. Harlow: Addison Wesley Longman.

Graves, Kathleen. 1993. 'The Teaching Game' in Freeman, Donald and Cornwell, Steve. *New Ways in Teacher Education*. TESOL: Alexandria, VA.

Grellet, Françoise. 1981. *Developing Reading Skills*. Cambridge: Cambridge University Press.

Greuber, Dianne and Dunn, Viviane. 1987. *Writing Elementary*. Oxford: Oxford University Press.

Grundy, Peter. 1993. *Newspapers*. Oxford: Oxford University Press.

Hadfield, Charles and Jill Hadfield. 1990. *Writing Games*. Harlow: Addison Wesley Longman.

Hadfield, Jill. 1992. *Classroom Dynamics*. Oxford: Oxford University Press.

Hadfield, Jill and Charles. 1995. *Reading Games*. Harlow: Addison Wesley Longman.

Hancock, Robert and David Settle. 1990. *Teacher Appraisal and Self-Evaluation*. Oxford: Basil Blackwell.

Harmer, Jeremy. 1987. *Teaching and Learning Grammar*. Harlow: Addison Wesley Longman.

Harmer, Jeremy. 1991 (New edition). *The Practice of English Language Teaching*. Harlow: Addison Wesley Longman.

Harris, M. and D. Mower. 1991. *World Class Level 2*. Harlow: Addison Wesley Longman.

Hedge, Tricia. 1988. *Writing*. Oxford: Oxford University Press.

Heron, John. 1992. *The Facilitator's Handbook*. London: Kogan Page

Hess, Nathalie. 1991. *Headstarts: One Hundred Original Pre-Text Activities*. Harlow: Pilgrims-Addison Wesley Longman.

Hill, David A. 1990. *Visual Impact*. Harlow: Pilgrims-Addison Wesley Longman.

Hinton, Michael and Paul Seligson. 1991. *Mosaic 1 and 2; Mosaic Teacher's Books 1 and 2*. Harlow: Addison Wesley Longman.

Holme, Randal. 1991. *Talking Texts*. Harlow: Pilgrims-Addison Wesley Longman.

Hopkins, David. 1985. *A Teacher's Guide to Classroom Research*. Milton Keynes: Open University Press.

Hopson, Barrie and Mike Scally. 1981. *Lifeskills Teaching*. London: McGraw-Hill.

Houston, Gaie. 1984. *The Red Book of Groups*. London: The Rochester Foundation.

Houston, Gaie. 1990. *Supervision and Counselling*. London: The Rochester Foundation.

Hutchings, Sue, Jayne Comins and Judy Offiler. 1991. *The Social Skills Handbook*. Bicester: Winslow Press.

Kirn, Elaine and Pamela Hartmann. 1985. *Interactions II: A Reading Skills Book*. Second edition. New York: McGraw-Hill, Inc.

Klippel, Friederike. 1984. *Keep Talking*. Cambridge: Cambridge University Press.

Krashen, Steven and Tracy Terrell. 1983. *The Natural Approach*. Oxford: Pergamon.

Lawley, Jim and Roger Hunt. 1992. *Fountain Beginners* and *Fountain Elementary*. Harlow: Addison Wesley Longman.

Lazar, Gillian. 1987. *Literature in the Language Classroom*. Cambridge: Cambridge University Press.

Long, Michael and Patricia Porter. 1985. 'Group work, interlanguage talk, and second language acquisition'. *TESOL Quarterly 19:2.*

Makino, Taka-Yoshi. 1993. 'Learner self-correction in EFL written compositions' in *ELT Journal 47 (4)* October, pp. 337-341.

Malamah-Thomas, Ann. 1987. *Classroom Interaction*. Oxford: Oxford University Press.

Maley, Alan and Alan Duff. 1989. *The Inward Ear: Poetry in the Language Classroom*. Cambridge: Cambridge University Press.

Morgan, John and Mario Rinvolucri. 1983. *Once Upon a Time*. Cambridge: Cambridge University Press.

Morgan, John and Mario Rinvolucri. 1986. *Vocabulary*. Oxford: Oxford University Press.

Moskowitz, Gertrude. 1976. *Caring and Sharing in the Foreign Language Class*. Cambridge, Massachusetts: Newbury House.

Murphey, Tim. 1992. *Music and Song*. Oxford: Oxford University Press.

Newstrom, John W and Edward E. Scannell. 1980. *Games Trainers Play*. New York: McGraw-Hill.

Nolasco, Rob and Lois Arthur. 1988. *Large Classes*. Hemel Hempstead: Prentice Hall International.

Nolasco, Rob and Lois Arthur. 1987. *Conversation*. Oxford: Oxford University Press.

Nolasco, Rob. 1987. *Writing Upper-Intermediate*. Oxford: Oxford University Press.

Nunan, David. 1995. *Language Teaching Methodology: A Textbook for Teachers*. Hemel Hempstead: Phoenix ELT.

Nunan, David. 1989. *Designing Tasks for the Communicative Classroom*. Cambridge: Cambridge University Press.

Nunan, David. 1989. *Understanding Language Classrooms: A Guide for Teacher-Initiated Action*. Hemel Hempstead: Prentice Hall International.

Nuttall, Christine. 1996. *Teaching Reading Skills in a Foreign Language*. Oxford: Heinemann.

Oller, John W., Jr., ed. 1993. *Methods that Work: Ideas for Literacy and Language Teachers*. Boston: Heinle and Heinle.

Oluwadiya, Adewumi. 1992. 'Some prewriting techniques for student writers'. *English Teaching Forum 30:4.* October. pp.12-15.

O'Neill, Helen and Jim Lawley. 1992. *Fountain Teacher's Book 1 Beginners*. Harlow: Addison Wesley Longman.

Oxford, Rebecca. 1990. *Language Learning Strategies: What Every Teacher Should Know*. Boston, Mass: Heinle and Heinle.

Parker, Sue. 'A question of planning'. *Practical English Teaching*. September 1990. p.25.

Pease, Allan. 1981. *Body Language*. London: Sheldon Press.

Peck, Antony. 1988. *Language Teachers at Work: A Description of Methods*. Englewood Cliffs, NJ: Prentice Hall, Inc.

Peyton, Joy Kreeft and Leslee Reed. 1990. *Dialogue Journal Writing with Non-native English Speakers: A Handbook for Teachers*. Alexandria, VA: TESOL.

Peyton, Joy Kreeft, ed. 1990. *Students and Teachers Writing Together: Perspectives on Journal Writing*. Alexandria, VA: TESOL.

Philpott, Patrick. 'The lesson planner's balancing act.' *Practical English Teaching*. June 1991. pp.21-22.

Porter, Patricia et al. 1990. 'An ongoing dialogue: learning logs for teacher preparation' in Richards and Nunan 1990.

Porter-Ladousse, Gillian. 1987. *Role Play*. Oxford: Oxford University Press.

Puchta, Herbert and Michael Schratz. 1993. *Teaching Teenagers*. Harlow: Pilgrims-Addison Wesley Longman.

Quirk, Randolph and Sidney Greenbaum. 1973. *A University Grammar of English*. Harlow: Addison Wesley Longman.

Radley, Paul and Chris Millerchip. 1990. *Mode 1, 2 and 3; Mode 1, 2 and 3 Teacher's Books*. Harlow: Addison Wesley Longman.

Raimes, Ann. 1983. *Techniques in Teaching Writing*. Oxford: Oxford University Press.

Reid, Joy, ed. 1995. *Learning Styles in the ESL/EFL Classroom*. Boston, Mass: Heinle and Heinle.

Richards, Jack C. and Charles Lockhart. 1994. *Reflective Teaching in Second Language Classrooms*. Cambridge: Cambridge University Press.

Richards, Jack C. and David Nunan, eds. 1990. *Second Language Teacher Education*. Cambridge: Cambridge University Press.

Richards, Jack C. with Jonathan Hull and Susan Proctor. 1991. *Interchange: English for International Communication*. Cambridge: Cambridge University Press.

Richards, Jack, John Platt and Heidi Weber. 1985. *The Longman Dictionary of Applied Linguistics*. Harlow: Addison Wesley Longman.

Rinvolucri, Mario and Paul Davis. 1988. *Dictation: New Methods, New Possibilities*. Cambridge: Cambridge University Press.

Rinvolucri, Mario and Paul Davis. 1995. *More Grammar Games*. Cambridge: Cambridge University Press

Rost, Michael. 1990. *Listening in Language Learning*. Harlow: Addison Wesley Longman.

Scarcella, Robin and Rebecca Oxford. 1992. *The Tapestry of Language Learning*. Boston, Mass: Heinle and Heinle.

Schön, Donald A. 1987. *Educating The Reflective Practitioner*. San Francisco: Jossey-Bass Publishers.

Shrum, Judith L. and Eileen W. Glisan. 1994. *Teacher's Handbook: Contextualized Language Instruction*. Boston, Mass: Heinle and Heinle.

Soars, John and Liz Soars. 1987. *Headway (Intermediate and Upper-Intermediate)*. Oxford: Oxford University Press.

Sokolik, Margaret E. 1993. *Global Views: Readings about World Issues*. Boston, Mass: Heinle and Heinle.

Stanford, Gene. 1990. *Developing Effective Classroom Groups*. Bristol: Acora Books.

Stevick, Earl W. 1976. *Memory, Meaning and Method*. Rowley, Mass: Newbury House.

Stevick, Earl W. 1980. *Teaching Languages: A Way and Ways*. Boston, Mass: Heinle and Heinle.

Stevick, Earl W. 1989. *Success With Foreign Languages*. New York: Prentice Hall International.

Swartz, Barbara Fowler and Richard. L. Smith. 1986. *This is a Recording: Listening with a Purpose*. Englewood Cliffs, N.J.: Prentice Hall, Inc.

Tuckman, Bruce W. 1965. 'Development Sequence in Small Groups'. *Psychological Bulletin 63:6*. pp. 384-399

Ur, Penny. 1981. *Discussions That Work*. Cambridge: Cambridge University Press.

Ur, Penny. 1984. *Teaching Listening Comprehension*. Cambridge: Cambridge University Press.

Ur, Penny. 1988. *Grammar Practice Activities*. Cambridge: Cambridge University Press.

Wajnryb, Ruth. 1992. *Classroom Observation Tasks: A Resource Book for Language Teachers and Trainers*. Cambridge: Cambridge University Press.

Wallace, Mike. 1991. *Training Foreign Language Teachers: A Reflective Approach*. Cambridge: Cambridge University Press.

Wenden, Anita. 1991. *Learner Strategies for Learner Autonomy*. Hemel Hempstead: Prentice Hall International.

Willis, Dave. 1991. *Collins Cobuild Student's Grammar*. London: HarperCollins.

Willis, Jane. 1981. *Teaching English Through English*. Harlow: Addison Wesley Longman.

Woodward, Tessa. 1992. *Ways of Training*. Harlow: Pilgrims-Addison Wesley Longman.

Woodward, Tessa and Seth Lindstromberg. 1995. *Planning from Lesson to Lesson: A Way of Making Lesson Planning Easier*. Harlow: Pilgrims-Addison Wesley Longman.

Woolcott, Lyn. 1992. *Take Your Pick*. Harlow: Addison Wesley Longman.

White, Ron. 1987. *Writing Advanced*. Oxford: Oxford University Press.

Wright, Tony. 1987. *Roles of Teachers and Learners*. Oxford: Oxford University Press.

Zamel, Vivian. 1985. 'Responding to student writing' in *TESOL Quarterly 19:1*. pp.79-101.

INDEX